It's Not Just You

MAKING SENSE OF LIFE AND THRIVING
AFTER GROWING UP IN AN
EMOTIONALLY DYSFUNCTIONAL FAMILY

Victoria Matthews-Patel

Putting Words
publishing

First published in 2022 by **Putting Words.**

© Victoria Matthews-Patel, 2022

The moral rights of the author have been asserted.

Putting Words
PO Box 5062
Wonga Park, Victoria, Australia. 3115
www.puttingwords.com
books@puttingwords.com

A catalogue record for this book is available from the National Library of Australia.

ISBN: 978-0-6454591-9-7 (eBook)
ISBN: 978-0-6456666-1-8 (Paperback)

Produced by **Putting Words**
Edited by Anna Von Zinner
Photos of Victoria taken by Kier Adair

It's Not Just You

Making Sense of Life and Thriving After Growing Up in an Emotionally Dysfunctional Family

"This is a must-read book for anyone who's at the beginning of their healing from emotional trauma, written by someone with immense insight, wisdom and compassion, who has found the route out of her complex PTSD, and wants to shine the light for others.

It's packed with excellent tips and tools from someone who really knows personally, the impact a lack of emotional attachment in childhood has on all aspects of life, and how to navigate successful recovery.

I wouldn't hesitate in recommending it. It's a fantastic addition to the emerging world of people starting to recognise and realise the widespread impact of trauma."

Lou Lebentz, Therapist, Trauma Specialist, EMDR Clinician, Transformational Speaker and Founder of Trauma Thrivers

"*It's Not Just You* is a book filled with hope and shame reducing strategies. Matthews-Patel's book is a must read for anyone looking to find their way through recovery from trauma after growing up in an emotionally dysfunctional family.

Bookstore shelves are filled with books written by clinicians on research and therapeutic tools to manage life after trauma. However, there are very few books written by life coaches who are also survivors themselves!

It's Not Just You is a guide that survivors of emotional trauma can incorporate into their therapy.

Matthews-Patel wrote a book that will leave readers feeling heard, seen and understood. I will be sharing this title with colleagues and clients for sure!"

Shari Botwin, LCSW author of
Thriving After Trauma: Stories of Living and Healing

For Ella.

I could not love you more

Acknowledgements

To Bups for supporting me in every way on my path to health and happiness. For your understanding, patience, and encouragement when I didn't think I could or would get better. For believing in me when I didn't. For your never-ending quest for tidiness. And for making me laugh. Laughter (and swearing!) has really helped me through. You rock.

To Ella. My wonderful, creative, adventurous and strong Ella. My inspiration to keep going every day. You lit up my world from the moment you were born. I am blessed to be your Mum.

To Murphy, my gorgeous dog, who witnessed more of my ill health than anyone. What a comfort and joy you are. A true companion and my little shadow.

To my beloved and much missed Uncle James who had love and joy oozing from him. I adored you. My memories of you will always make me smile.

To my Gran. My no-nonsense, strong Gran with her wicked sense of humour and her love of cake.

Sometimes we need guides in life. People to help us through. People who see in us the things we can't see in ourselves. People who give us hope and direction.

I am blessed to have truly wonderful women as my guides.

To Abi Briant-Smith, Lori Fitzgerald, Katharine Haworth, Shushana Smith and Michelle Taylor-Ward. Your impact on my life has been incredible. I would not be the person I am today without you all. Keep shining.

To Lou Lebentz and Mel Curtis of Trauma Thrivers for your kindness, passion and inspiration. For spreading the word about trauma and its impact.

I am grateful to all who have been friends at different ages and stages of my life.

To the "Awesome Women" who I am blessed to have as friends - Jayne Holliday, Nicki Margand, Nicki Mitchinson, Sarah Owen-Hughes, Janey Sharp and Louise Thatch. Our weekend together, beautifully organised by Lou, was very special. You raise me up.

To friends Caron Page, Clare Sewell and Clare Waterer, for your care and your compassion.

To the "Safe Space" women who got me through the darkest times. You know who you are. I will be forever grateful to you.

To Lorna Dunning, my cousin and coach, who helped me navigate my way from a feeling of hopelessness to this exciting new chapter in my life. You helped me see my value again. Thank you from the bottom of my heart.

To my writing cheerleader and book cover consultant, Nicki Mitchinson. Thank you for encouraging me to speak up, share my story and write. "From being inspired to being inspiring......"

To Anna Von Zinner, my writing coach and editor, for guiding me through the book mapping and writing process. This book would not have been written without your direction and encouragement.

To Andrea Putting for guiding me through the publishing process and keeping me motivated when my confidence wavered.

Empowered women empower women.

I am so proud of this book.

Thank you to everyone who played a part in inspiring me and encouraging me to write it.

With Compassion,

Victoria xx

Contents

Chapter Three

Chapter Four

Chapter 5

Chapter Six

Chapter Seven

Chapter Eight

Chapter Nine

Moving from People-Pleasing to Setting Boundaries

Chapter Ten

Chapter Eleven

Chapter Twelve

Introduction

"Thank God for books, for validating your feelings, and letting you know you're not alone."

Paula Gruben, Umbilicus

No-one gets "it".

You try to talk to people about "it" but no-one has experienced "it".

You feel bad.

You can't make sense of "it".

You retreat.

You hide.

Life feels painful.

You bring up memories with your childhood family and your reality is questioned or dismissed. They can't understand why you are bringing up past events.

You go inside your head to try to make sense of things, but the pain is too much.

You try to put "it" to the back of your mind and get on with your life, but "it" keeps resurfacing.

You don't know what to do.

You can't seem to move on, to let "it" go. Those memories won't go away.

You are in a never-ending cycle of confusion, emptiness, and shame.

It starts to tear you apart.

You feel like you are breaking from the inside out.

I didn't know exactly what "it" was, but I knew that something was wrong.

I felt like I was the only one who had gone through "it".

Thinking that you are the only one is lonely. Very lonely.

It can feel like you're in the wrong, that you are imagining it, that it wasn't that bad, that you are being oversensitive, that you deserved what happened, that it happened because there is something wrong with you.

The sense of confusion can be overwhelming.

Maybe there were happy times in the family. Maybe you had a good education, holidays etc. But there were distressing and confusing times too. Times that made you change who you were to keep the peace. Times that made you question yourself. Times that were never talked about or explained. Times where you needed comfort, reassurance and emotional support, but they were not forthcoming. Times that left you feeling lonely and confused.

My definition of an emotionally dysfunctional family is one in which:

- Belittling, criticism, and control are seen as an acceptable part of the family dynamic.
- Difficult events aren't talked about.

- There is a sense of unease or of walking on eggshells.
- Emotions aren't welcomed or acknowledged.
- You find it hard to speak freely.
- There is a lack of unconditional love and emotional support.
- Family members have roles – black sheep, golden child, enabler etc.
- Family members are seen as responsible for the happiness of others within the family.
- Family members are expected to follow family norms.
- Being 'different' to the family norm is not acceptable and is seen as a threat to the family dynamic.
- You hear judgement and criticism of other people – the narrative that 'they' are all wrong and 'we' are right.
- You are fed the narrative that you are from a 'good' and 'close' family.

In this book I want you to know that you are not alone. That "It's Not Just You."

This is the book I wish I had when I felt broken and couldn't see a way forward. When I was confused, hurting, and didn't know where to turn.

This book will show you a way forward if you're struggling to make sense of it all.

Although it describes my experiences, it is a book for you.

I want you to know that it's not just you.

I want you to know that:

- I hear you.

- I see you.
- You matter.

You are important.

You have ALWAYS been enough.

I want you to know that there is the possibility of happiness, joy and thriving after everything that happened.

Each chapter goes through a different stage that I went through in the process of making sense of my life.

Woven into the book are personal experiences in my healing with information and tips for you.

I don't want to overload or overwhelm you, so there is a list of additional books and resources that I invite you to access when you feel ready.

I include quotes at the end of each chapter as quotes were important to me during my healing. I had different quotes at different stages of my healing and often referred to them to keep me going.

Before you read the book, I want you to know that no-one has the right to treat you badly, irrespective of how they were treated, what happened to them in the past and who they are in your life.

Being family does not give a person permission to belittle, judge, control or bully you.

This book is not about my family or your family – see the additional reading section for some useful books about families.

This book is about you; helping you to make sense of your life and to understand why you adopted certain behaviours to cope with what happened.

It is about getting to know and value the real you, who got lost at different stages of your life.

I am a Compassionate Coach and Mentor. I am not a trauma specialist, but at the time of writing, I am training to become a trauma-informed coach.

A trauma is a distressing event where you feel scared, unsafe, rejected, humiliated, invalidated, unsupported, powerless or ashamed, and how you are affected by it. Trauma is personal and traumatic events can cause long-lasting harm to your health, thought processes and behaviours. The effects can happen quickly or a long time afterwards. Lack of emotional attachment in childhood is trauma. It's about what happened as well as what was lacking.

I have Complex Post Traumatic Stress Disorder (CPTSD) due to lack of emotional attachment in childhood and am not just living after trauma, but thriving.

At the time of writing this book my healing is four years and ongoing.

Speaking up about my experience, seeking professional help, connecting with others who have been through something similar, and telling my story, although challenging and scary, has changed my life for the better.

I hope that sharing my story helps you feel less alone.

With Compassion,

Victoria

October 2022

"That story you're afraid to tell will be a lifeline of hope for someone who is hurting and afraid they're the only one."

Nate Postlethwait
@nate_postlethwait on Instagram

Eight Tips for "It's Not Just You."

1. If you are feeling overwhelmed, go carefully. Maybe one or two pages at a time. You may want to make notes and come back to the book later when you have had the chance to reflect.
2. You may find you forget what you are reading and need to read sections/chapters a few times. There is repetition in the book as revisiting things was important on my healing journey.
3. The book's format allows clear opportunities for breaks for reflection or further research.
4. There are tips at the end of each chapter.
5. There is an additional resources section at the back of the book containing a list of books and social media accounts that I found helpful. You may wish to access some of these to find out more.
6. If you feel triggered or overwhelmed, take a break from the book and come back to it when you feel ready.
7. Always be compassionate with yourself. There is no timeframe for healing work. It is a daily and ongoing practice.
8. Speak to a close and safe person/people and reach out for professional help to guide you through.

Disclaimer – Reading this book may trigger you to past events. If you feel overwhelmed or experience any mental distress, I recommend informing a Doctor or mental health professional.

If you are currently in a difficult or violent domestic situation, please consult a specialist if taking any of the actions suggested in the book could be dangerous for you, for example setting boundaries.

Your safety is always the number one priority.

CHAPTER ONE

Something's Not Right

Have you gone through life feeling something isn't quite right? You don't know what it is. You can't put your finger on it. But something about your life is off. It's always in the back of your mind. Maybe it occasionally comes to the forefront of your mind, but you can't work it out.

The most important thing to say here and now is that I hear you.

I've been there too. I had a recurring theme in my head of things not being okay and that there was something wrong with me.

My first step in making sense of how I felt was to explore online and read. I have read self-development books all my adult life, but I always focused on myself and what I thought was wrong with me. I didn't focus outwards on the impact others in my life had on me.

I started with a correspondence course (yes, a course that came through the mail!) on being an introvert and shy when I was at university in the late 1980s. I read further about social anxiety, lack of confidence, low self-esteem, being highly sensitive, and being an empath for the next 30 years.

I read one self-help book after another, hoping each one would "cure me", that each one would make me happy and help me work myself out, but to no avail. After finishing each book, I would go further down the negative spiral, feeling worse about myself because none of the books seemed to get me or to help me feel better.

It took until my late 40s to realise the problem wasn't me. It was what happened to me.

I had been focusing on my perceived flaws all my life. It had been about me and everything that was wrong with me, and there was a lot. There wasn't much I liked about myself.

During my 40s, lots of difficult memories came back.

I tried to process the memories in my head, but again and again I came back to thinking that there were faults with me. There was something wrong with ME. I was the problem.

Having my daughter changed my life. Having her made me realise I could not treat her in the same way I was treated as a child and during adulthood.

Memories from my childhood came up during the different stages of her childhood. Memories that got me thinking back to things I knew weren't right. Things I knew I needed to delve into deeply.

I thought something about my family wasn't right, but I didn't know what. At various stages of my life, I had chatted to people about my experiences, but none of them seemed to know what I meant. I felt lonely and isolated. I couldn't put my finger on it, but no one else seemed to have gone through something similar.

I internalised everything. I went inside my head and tried to make sense of things.

Trying to work it out took its toll. How can anyone else get you when you don't get yourself? My feelings of despair lead to further isolation, self-loathing and even self-contempt.

I started slowly but surely to back away from being with my childhood family as I tried to process things. I began to think about how I felt when I was around them. I didn't feel good. I felt drained. I shut down, but I didn't know why. The stress and anxiety I felt around them were intense at times.

My Breakdown

In August 2018, I had a breakdown after years of declining physical and mental health.

2018 had been a difficult year at work. I was overworking to prove my worth and to get some form of acknowledgement, that was never going to come. At the end of one particularly horrible day – a day that ended up being my last working day for nearly two years - my heart started pounding, my arms were tight, my head was in so much pain. I remember pacing around the house thinking I was going mad. I thought I was dying from a heart attack. I felt like I couldn't go on.

I had reached a point of no return. I knew I had to do something. I knew I was the only person who could do anything to improve my life. My head was full of pain and dark thoughts. I also thought I was weak. I thought weakness had caused my breakdown. I thought that this would not have happened to me if I had been stronger.

"Depressive Illness – The Curse of the Strong"

I reached out to a friend, who suggested I read a particular chapter in the book, *Depressive Illness – The Curse of the Strong* by Dr Tim Cantopher. This book sent me such an important message – that this hadn't happened because I was weak. It was the complete opposite. My breakdown had happened because I was strong. I had been trying to be strong for so many people for so long.

"Give a set of stresses to someone who is weak, cynical or lazy and he will quickly give up...... A strong person, on the other hand, will react to these pressures by trying to overcome them. ....she keeps going, absorbing more and more until, inevitably, symptoms emerge. At this point most people would say 'Hang on, this is ridiculous, I'm doing too much, I'm getting symptoms! You're going to have to help'.......But the sensitive person, without a very solid sense of self-esteem, can't stop struggling, because she fears others being disappointed in her. Even more than this she feels disappointed in herself........So she keeps going, on and on and on, until suddenly: BANG! The fuse blows."

Cantopher describes the personality characteristics of the type of person that depression affects – they were all me! I hadn't "seen" myself described in a book before.

He also describes the insular, unhappy child that I was. The me that I had been trying to work out all my adult life.

"It isn't your fault. The problem comes from your background, not from any failing of yours," Cantopher writes.

Maybe it wasn't me all these years. Many statements in Cantopher's book jolted me, giving me some hope after years of feeling weak and like I always had to prove myself.

Just reading this changed things for me. Suddenly, I wasn't blaming myself. I wasn't weak. I was strong. This was life-changing. I felt like I wasn't on my own for the first time. Other people had gone through this. Dr Cantopher helped me feel seen after years of feeling like the only one. I didn't know these people but knowing they were out there brought some solace.

Reading this chapter helped me realise I wasn't alone. I wasn't the only one having dark times, physical symptoms, anxiety, overwhelming thoughts, and working myself into the ground to get respect.

I continued to read. I wanted to understand what had happened to me. There must be a way to get through it. Life had to be better than this. Life hurt. Life was painful. I wanted to understand why this breakdown had happened. I didn't want to accept things as they were. It was as if the breakdown was a catalyst to say, "No more. This cannot go on".

I wanted to get better. I also wanted someone to understand me, but I also wanted to understand myself. I had been trying to work myself out for years. After years of thinking I was flawed, I wanted to truly understand myself.

Over the coming months, I extended my reading based on my recovery and healing. Sometimes I would take a break in my reading as it got too much. My head was pounding, and the thoughts were never-ending. I took breaks until I had the headspace to continue.

My advice is that when you begin your journey of discovery, always take things at your pace. There is no rush. You need to protect and look after yourself. This is hard. Things may come up that hurt, that sting, that make you take a backwards step. Treat yourself with kindness and compassion always. The most important person in all of this is you.

This work takes time, so please be gentle and proceed at the right pace for you.

"The Joy of Burnout"

The next life-changing book for me was recommended to me at a women's circle, where women connected and shared life stories. The book was *The Joy of Burnout - How the End of the World Can Be a New Beginning* by Dr Dina Glouberman.

Burnout did not describe what had happened to me. I had broken down. I felt broken, but this book gave me the hope that good things could come from this. A breakdown wasn't the end of the world; a breakdown was the opportunity for change.

Language is important – not a breakdown, but a breakthrough. It could be a positive thing. The book gave me glimmers of hope and optimism. Hearing someone else say breaking down was the impetus for a renewed life gave me hope. Maybe things could change. Maybe my life could improve. Maybe I could feel happy again. All these "maybes" spurred me on.

"Dodging Energy Vampires"

The next book that resonated through Google searching was *Dodging Energy Vampires – an Empath's Guide to Evading*

Relationships that Drain You and Restoring your Health and Power by Christine Northrup M.D.

I read this book, and it helped me connect with how I felt when I was around certain people in my life. It helped me process feelings I encountered when I spent time with these people – the literal draining of energy and enthusiasm I felt in their presence – that feeling of anxiety at having to spend time with them.

I felt compelled to be around these people because they are family members. This book helped me understand things a little better. I started to connect with how I felt around different people.

Did these people radiate warmth in me? Did they uplift me? Or did they drain me? Did they leave me feeling bad about myself? It was difficult to realise that I had been giving most of my energy to vampires and that some of these vampires were in my family. They sucked the energy out of me.

Where were my radiators? I wanted to spend more time with the people who gave me the warmth and energy I needed.

I continued to read. This was helping me start to unravel things in my mind. Next, I read some books about narcissism. Some aspects resonated, and some didn't.

"Adult Children of Emotionally Immature Parents"

Then after some online research, I came across the book, *Adult Children of Emotionally Immature Parents – How to Heal from*

Distant, Rejecting, or Self-Involved Parents by Lindsay C. Gibson. This was THE book for me. It was full of "that was me", "that was my family", and "that happened to me" moments. I felt heard and seen.

Someone else has gone through this. This author understood what my family life was like. This author gets me. There are other families out there like mine. There are people out there who feel like me and have been through similar experiences.

Unsurprisingly, my copy of the book is full of post-it notes and underlinings, and I wrote copious notes in the margins. It was the start of me making sense of my life. I was starting to see that it wasn't me all this time. It was what had happened and was still happening to me. I realised how emotionally lonely I was and had been since childhood.

"Emotionally immature parents can have devastating impacts on their children's self-esteem and relationships in adulthood. The effects can range from mild to severe, depending on the parent's level of immaturity, but the net effect is the same: the children feel emotionally unseen and lonely. This erodes the child's sense of their own lovability and can lead to excessive caution about emotional intimacy with others."

Lindsay C. Gibson,
Adult Children of Emotionally Immature Parents – How to Heal from Distant, Rejecting, or Self-Involved Parents

I had a mental list of difficult people in my life, and some of them were people who should have been my biggest cheerleaders. I encountered others, mainly women, who treated me in a similar way. People who didn't want to see me, didn't value me, and sometimes belittled/mistreated/bullied/tried to control me.

But some women didn't treat me this way. This confused me. Maybe some women were okay. Perhaps it wasn't me, but it must be me because it was ongoing and kept happening. I felt like I couldn't get on with women.

Can you sense the inner turmoil that was going on? The common factor was me, so I must be the problem. It was all my fault. I had carried this with me all my life. I felt like I didn't fit in my family and came to realise that I had been searching to belong somewhere all my life.

When the people who should be your champions aren't, you believe them. You don't take it out on them. You internalise it and take it out on yourself without realising it. You believe that those in a position of care or authority must be right, and you continually diminish yourself. You make yourself invisible. You turn into a people pleaser and someone who puts themselves last. The level of self-loathing is intense and extremely difficult to describe.

Maybe this is something you are experiencing too. If so, be gentle and compassionate with yourself. Read and make notes. See what comes up, but please share what you are doing with someone who is a safe person for you. When I say safe, I mean emotionally safe. Someone who doesn't just listen, but someone who also hears you. Someone who can hear what you are saying without trying to diminish it or justify it. Someone who doesn't judge, who doesn't try to make sense of it. You can't make sense of it yourself, so why would they be able to?

Your Experience

You are the only one who knows your experience within your family. Even though you are in the same family and living in the same house growing up, your experiences and feelings are different and unique to you.

Dr Gabor Mate, psychologist and author, spoke at an online event I attended recently, Trauma: A Path to Self-Realisation. He said that no two children within the same family have the same experience of their parents. This is because the children have different temperaments and evoke different things in their parents. How a child is treated can be affected by gender, birth order, expectations etc, as well as the mental state of the parents. One child's experience within the family can be quite different to another's.

This was powerful for me as I often had my experiences questioned or played down by my family.

Start to Share, Read and Explore

Find someone who can hold the space for you whilst you share what is coming up. Don't try to get through this alone but check they are okay to listen to whatever comes up for you. What comes up may be just as hard for them to process as it is for you. You may be telling them difficult things they didn't know about someone in your life that they also have a relationship with.

Reach out. Start with books. Start exploring. If something didn't feel right in your life, explore. Try not to internalise it and turn against yourself. Look at the situation – what happened? Can you make sense of it? How did your younger self react? Looking back with what you know now, what does your adult self-think about what happened?

A word of caution, though – don't go into a book expecting to see yourself as this could lead to negative feelings. Be open and see if anything within the book resonates. Don't give up if it doesn't. There may just be one element in the book, maybe just one statement, that leads you to feel seen.

Starting to Feel Connected Through Books

Reading can create a feeling of connection. You are not connecting with anyone directly, but the author's words make you feel visible, perhaps for the first time in your life. It's like someone taking you into a giant bear hug. Someone else understands you and what happened to you.

This is the first of many steps but such an important start to reaching out and feeling that connection you have perhaps lacked and missed but always wanted. It may be the missing piece in the jigsaw of your life. You no longer feel quite so alone.

There is an innate power in seeing yourself described in a book. By seeing yourself described by others, you start to feel seen. Self-confidence comes from knowing the truth of your story.

"We read to know we are not alone."

C.S. Lewis

Seven Tips for Making Sense of Things When Reading

1. Start to explore. Put keywords into an online search engine.
2. Look for book recommendations backed up by scientific research and read articles by professional therapists and counsellors etc.
3. Take your time when you read. Concentration is affected by anxiety and depression.
4. Things might affect you profoundly, so give yourself time to absorb what you are reading and go at the pace that works for you.
5. Take breaks for your mental health. There is no timeframe for this work.
6. Don't give up if one book doesn't have the impact you were hoping for. Even if there are only a few statements within the whole book that resonate, this is a start. There will be another book out there for you.
7. Know that there is a way forward and keep going. Always be kind and compassionate with yourself and seek professional support if you are feeling overwhelmed.

CHAPTER TWO

The Power of Writing

You are reading. You are starting to see yourself in books. You are discovering that it's not just you. You are beginning to understand. What next?

My advice – WRITE! Make notes, lots of notes. Write a journal describing the experiences and feelings coming up, and get the thoughts out of your head.

If you don't like writing, you can record yourself talking through things and listen back to them. Speak into your phone and let the phone do the writing.

Writing, or getting things out, helps to release the mental blocks. It allows you to reflect. It gives you a break from the reading – a time to pause, think and sit with what is coming up for you. Emotions will undoubtedly come up, and you need time to process them.

Writing eases the pressure on your overthinking mind that is feeling the pain of the memories returning. Write about the pain. Write about the emotions you are feeling but also how it feels in your body. For example, do your shoulders stiffen as you remember past events. Do your jaws tighten? Do you get any pains in your body?

Write about the whole experience, both the mental and the physical.

When you write, the focus is now on you and what happened to you. Before, you may have focused on the other people and what they said and did. You may have internalised it and blamed things on yourself. This is the time for you to connect with how things felt for you.

You will feel further connected with the author of the book you are reading when what they write about resonates with your life. Write about that feeling of connection. How does it make you feel? Do you feel seen and heard? Do you feel visible for the first time in your life? Is there a feeling of, "It's not just me"?

As you write, you might feel you want to reach out and get support from a professional. There is only so much you can deal with on your own. This is difficult work. You may be bringing back memories that have been stored away for years. You may be remembering things that really hurt you.

Getting Support

Start to research the support you need so that you can take action when it feels right for you. Research your options. You may wish to go to a doctor for advice or for a referral to a specialist.

Do your research if you need support more urgently and are going down the private route. Rapport is essential in such a close relationship. The most important thing is feeling comfortable and emotionally safe with the person you will be speaking to about things you may never have talked about before. This is important and emotionally challenging work, and you want it to be with someone you feel safe with and who you can trust.

There is more information on Seeking Professional Support in Chapter 6.

Why Write?

There are many reasons for writing.

Writing gets your thoughts out of your head and onto paper. It gives you some headspace given everything that is coming up for you.

Writing helps you remember the lightbulb moments you are experiencing as you connect with authors and with experiences in the books you read.

Keeping a paper trail as you read helps you track back. The more you read, the more things make sense, but you may need to reread. Noting down your lightbulb moments – the book and the page number – makes this process easier. You could regard this as an academic project in which you are noting down quotes that you know you will have to refer back to. This saves you the frustration of having to track back through a book to find the information you know you have seen somewhere!

If you come across a book that resonates strongly, look to see if that author is on social media. If they are, follow them. Connecting can lead to further discovery and further insights into your life. But be careful not to get too absorbed in the pain, suffering and experience of others. You have enough to contend with.

If something comes up in your head, write it down. Some days the thoughts will pour out, and you won't be able to type or write fast enough. On other days little will come. Be kind and compassionate with yourself. This is okay. You may feel stuck some days. Some days you will need a break from the reading and the writing, just to be. This can be overwhelming work.

You could write in a journal; you could write on your computer or a device. But write in a way that you know where your notes are. Scattered notes all over the place create disharmony at a time when you may already be feeling emotionally fragile and scattered.

People throughout history have documented their experiences through diaries or journals. They wrote what was happening in real-time. Those diaries have proved to be incredible resources of human emotion, suffering, and experience.

Journalling

Journal or diary writing is an effective way of managing what is happening and helping you process the range of emotions and behaviours coming up for you.

Journalling allows you to express your feelings, experiences and most importantly, your insights − what you are learning and gaining from your reading.

Journalling promotes deep insight and self-awareness. It can lead to massive changes as you try to make sense of what happened to you. It may feel jumbled at first, but the more you read and write, the more sense it will begin to make.

Journalling can offer comfort. You may find that you look forward to that moment when you can write. Writing or getting your thoughts out of your head can be cathartic. It can feel like an emotional and physical release.

Your Inner Voice

You may have had an inner voice for a long time. Let that inner voice speak to you and record the words on paper. Your inner voice speaks to you regularly and wants you to know something.

The inner voice might be an inner critic, which you can thank and tell kindly to shush if it gets too much. It might be a younger version of you letting you know what they need, or what they needed back at the stage of your life when difficult things happened.

When writing you can reflect on yourself, the other people involved, your experiences, and your memories. This writing is just for you. No one is reading or judging what you have written.

Your writing is intensely personal and therapeutic. These are your experiences. You are writing about how these experiences affected you and their impact on you, perhaps over a very long period. No one is reading your writing, so no one can deny your reality and deny or try to diminish your experience. This gives you ownership and power.

Your Story

This is YOUR story, and this might be the first time you have told it. This might be the first time you have felt strong or brave enough to write it, or maybe this is the beginning of unravelling a lifetime of distress. Go easy and take breaks but write when you can.

Own the uniqueness of your story.

Even within the same family, we all experience things differently. We are all different characters and personalities and view the world through our own unique lens. You may have been raised to look at the world through the lens of a particular member of your family who wanted you to put their needs before your own or to look through the lens of men, your culture or society. This is your chance to write about things through your unique lens and from your perspective.

You may be from a family where difficult, dysfunctional or toxic experiences were never discussed, things that have been stored inside you ever since they occurred. Situations you could not understand or process, so this confusion has been within your body for years. Things that you thought you had forgotten but that have always been there.

"I want to write a novel about Silence, he said; the things people don't say."

Virginia Woolf

You don't need to be silent anymore. Others in your family may not have been able to speak about and acknowledge what happened, but this is your chance to express it in words. Your chance to get out your confusion, distress, sadness, anger or whatever came up for you that you had to push back inside.

Other family members may have denied your reality. They may have viewed the same experiences differently. This does not make your experiences wrong. No one can deny how something made you feel. Your feelings are important, and this may be the first time you have been able to own and express them. Don't hold back.

You may have spent years trying to work yourself out. You may have spent years berating yourself for your perceived flaws. You may have turned what happened to you inwards and told yourself that you are the issue.

By writing things down, you begin to see yourself as a mistreated human being. A human being that didn't deserve what happened to them. A human being that has feelings, wants and needs. A human being who is important and deserves to be valued.

There are times in life when we naturally become reflective. This could be when you have a child and reflect on your childhood. Being with your child at different ages and stages brings back memories. Some of them might be painful.

Women become very reflective during their midlife years.

"You probably know about hot flushes but, the most powerful menopausal changes centre around your identity, who you are, and what kind of person you long to be."

Kate Codrington,
Second Spring: The Self-Care Guide to the Menopause.

We look back at our life so far during midlife and wonder what next? Do I want to go on living this way? Do I want a change in my life? What is hindering me from moving forwards? How am I feeling? Do I feel good about my life? Lots of questions come up, and we find ourselves reflecting and questioning.

This is when memories surface. As Kate Codrington writes, "Wounds and trauma we have shoved under the carpet for years emerge for healing."

We may find that while we would have stuffed those difficult memories away before, we now want to go there, or there is an overwhelming feeling that we must go there. We don't want life to continue as it is. Life cannot continue as it is. We are hurting, but we don't know why. Channelling these thoughts into writing is a good start.

Writing

"Writing – even sloppy, distraught writing – requires your brain activity to move out of the primitive emotional centres and route itself up through the higher, frontal parts of the brain where language, meaning and insight live. As far as the brain is concerned, your writing is an evolutionary stage above your feeling."

Lindsay C. Gibson,
Self-Care for Adult Children of Emotionally Immature Parents.

The Harvard Health report, *Writing About Emotions May Ease Stress and Trauma* states, "Writing helps people to organise thoughts and give meaning to a traumatic experience."

"...... when people open up privately about a traumatic event, they are more likely to talk with others about it — suggesting that writing leads indirectly to reaching out for social support that can aid healing."

Reading and writing are both important factors on your road to self-discovery and future connection.

I have always loved writing. Well, that isn't entirely true. I have always loved writing a diary, journalling and writing a blog, even before they were a thing! I rarely enjoyed writing stories or the school version of writing a story. The thought of having to be creative filled me with horror. A lack of confidence and feelings of anxiety hampered my creativity. But I could write about real life and feelings and loved doing it. It helped me process things too.

I have written daily since I was young. I have always been a diary writer, journalling the angst of my teenage years, trying to work myself out by getting my thoughts out onto paper, journalling my daughter's life, writing about the incredible challenge of my 40s etc.

I have lots of notebooks, diaries and journals full of memories. It can be difficult reading back about challenging times in my life, but it can also be hugely joyful to be reminded so vividly about stages in my daughter's life. Things that I may have forgotten otherwise, and those memories make my heart sing.

Some days I couldn't keep up with my thoughts as I wrote. Some days I had nothing to write. I didn't force it. I wrote when it felt like the right thing for me. This is key. Don't force it. Write when you get the urge to and the words will flow. If it doesn't flow, stop. If it hurts too much, stop. If you are not in the right frame of mind, stop. Don't berate yourself. It wasn't meant to happen at that point.

Some days I wrote as if I was writing a blog. Some days I wrote notes. There are no rules. This writing is for you. Write as you see fit. You don't need to produce the perfect piece of writing. (It doesn't exist, by the way!) You don't need punctuation, and you don't need to write neatly – as long as you can read it, everything's okay! This writing is by you and for you. It is for your eyes only, unless you decide to share in the future, and this is your choice.

Four years on from my breakdown I still write often. If I wake up during the night troubled by thoughts, I write. I continue to write a journal and to write about subjects that interest me.

So, my advice is to write. Write freely. Don't worry about making sense. Don't worry about what others may think. You have free rein over this. This is your chance – possibly your first chance – to tell your story.

Maya Angelou wrote, "There is no greater agony than bearing an untold story inside of you."

When you have finished each piece of writing, it is up to you what you do with it. You may want to keep it. You may wish to refer to it again. Conversely, you may want to shred it or delete it. It is your choice. If I feel particularly pained by something, or need to get anger out, I write my feelings down and then I destroy the piece of paper.

Offer yourself compassion during and after the writing process. Sit and offer yourself some compassionate touch. I put two hands to my heart to provide comfort and compassion, but you may prefer to put your face in your hands, give yourself a hug, or lean your head on your shoulder. Have a warm drink. Sit and cuddle your pet, if you have one! Go for a walk in nature. Do something calming to soothe yourself.

And always remember to celebrate your strength and bravery. This is hard work, but you are doing it.

"Putting the contents of your mind down on paper should be in every home's first aid manual as the best response to overwhelming situations. It is the single most effective self-help method you can use when circumstances have outrun your ability to keep up."

Lindsay C. Gibson, PsyD,
Self-Care for Adult Children of Emotionally Immature Parents

Nine Tips for Writing

1. Make notes as you read – write down those statements that scream out at you, help you feel seen, and make you think, "that's me".
2. Start to get things out of your head by writing.
3. Get your thoughts out in whatever form works best for you – notebook, notes on your device, speaking into your phone and the phone writing the text. You could record yourself speaking sometimes.
4. Only write when it feels right. Don't force it.
5. Take your time. Take breaks. Look after you.
6. If it feels too much, it is too much for you at that point. Stop. Come back to it when it feels right again. Be compassionate with yourself.
7. Get it all out. No filters, no editing. Write from the heart.
8. After you finish writing, take time to soothe yourself in whatever way is best for you
9. Celebrate your courage and your strength. You are amazing.

CHAPTER THREE

Reaching Out and Connecting on Social Media

Things may be starting to make more sense through your reading and writing. You may feel more confused at times. A whole range of emotions could be coming up as you do this work. There is no right or wrong way for this work to happen.

You may be starting to see that others feel like you. Others have had similar experiences to you. Others are hurting like you. Others may have blamed themselves as you do. Although you are not yet directly connecting with anyone, there is a feeling of connection. A sense of "it's not just me" or "someone else out there knows what it's like".

At this stage, you may feel like you are ready to reach out. This may be to a professional, and I urge you to seek professional help when it feels right. Only you will know when that time is. You will feel it. Let your head and your heart guide you.

Your reading and writing may lead you to follow experts in the field on social media. You may be reading these experts' posts and gaining further insight. You may see other social media posts that offer more insight into your past.

Research these experts. What expertise and experience do they have?

It is crucial to protect yourself online.

One of the most crucial aspects of this work is safety – feeling safe, emotionally safe. This work could cause further hurt and distress if you don't feel safe.

What is Emotional Safety?

You may never have heard of emotional safety before. I hadn't.

When you feel emotionally safe, you connect with others.

When you feel emotionally safe, you feel relaxed, open and able to express yourself.

When you feel emotionally safe, you are absorbed in what you are doing. You are not overthinking; you are not feeling on edge.

So, how do you know when you feel emotionally safe around someone?

You feel uplifted.

You feel good.

You feel positive.

You feel at ease.

You are living in the present moment.

Engaging on Social Media

Consider your emotional safety when you engage on social media.

At first, you may just want to scroll and read.

Then – and you will know when the time is right – you may decide you want to actively engage with others.

Often, it can feel easier to open up to someone you don't know than it is to "your people".

When I say "your people", I mean any close and supportive family and friends, etc.

On the Kripalu website Peter A. Levine writes, "Trauma is about broken connections. Connection is broken with the body/self, family, friends, community, nature and spirit. Healing trauma is about restoring these connections."

It can feel hard to connect and speak up. The fear of being judged, of hearing others' opinions, of not being believed, of invalidation, of being diminished can be overwhelming and can shut us down.

It can feel easier to reach out to strangers online. We may not know them, but they may get what we are going through as they have been through something similar. Shared experience and common humanity create connections. A connection can help life seem manageable, hopeful and possible again.

When I met someone who had gone through something similar to me, things really started to change for the better. It wasn't just me.

When you feel ready, connect with other people in the same situation. There seems to be a Facebook group for everything these days, so do your research. Have a look for any private groups linked to your circumstances. Who runs these groups, and how are they moderated? Read the rules around the group, especially in terms of confidentiality.

Join Facebook groups run by professionals, as things can still be raw for you. Be mindful of your mental health so that you don't start to absorb or feel compelled to comment on other people's pain and experiences. Seeing posts from others in a similar situation might feel overwhelming for you so check in with yourself about how you are feeling. Act on what comes up. Trust your intuition. You don't have to post a reply.

Many people who have survived trauma go on to work in the field. They want to help others. They want others to know there is a way forward. There is a way of not only living after the trauma but thriving. Seeing these possibilities could be overwhelming – you may not believe that you will ever get to that stage – or it could inspire you to keep going. Journal what comes up. Know that it is possible to move on from trauma and thrive after it but that it takes time and commitment.

Someone on social media may post something that will give you a moment of pure relief. The "It's not just me" lightbulb moment helps you feel seen.

After being in a group for a while, you might feel ready to dip that toe in. If you are nervous or anxious, practise writing your words on paper first. Read your comments and then re-read them. Does it feel right? If it does, give it a go. Post your words and see how you feel after you have done it. If it doesn't feel right, you can always delete it.

Someone may want to reach out to you and connect personally. You don't have to do this if you don't want to. Always do what feels right for you.

In my experience, there can be less judgment within private-focused social media groups. On the whole, you are in a group with people who have gone through something similar and understand you, and you don't have to explain yourself. That feeling of emotional freedom can be magical.

But do connect with yourself to see how you feel when interacting with others.

- Does it feel good?
- Do you feel better afterwards?
- Do you feel safe?

Ask yourself these questions regularly, and heed your responses. You can journal your thoughts.

Stop when things get too much.

If you feel overwhelmed with the number of posts, you can change the settings on Facebook, so you don't see any notifications from the group. You can look at posts within the group when it is right for you.

Take a break from the group when you need to.

If things feel too much or if it doesn't feel right, leave the group.

This work can be overwhelming.

"An integral part of healing from trauma is finding a way to trust yourself and those around you."

Shari Botwin,
Thriving After Trauma, Stories of Living and Healing.

Because of what happened to you, and if you heard dismissals from the people involved when you raise past incidents, you might not trust yourself or others. You may not trust your version of events because others have questioned what you have said in the past or because they told you that your memory of the experience is wrong.

This lack of trust contributes to your not feeling confident in connecting, but when it feels right, try it and see how it feels.

Scrolling through social media, you may also see some posts that sting.

Toxic Positivity

Positive vibes only.

Don't worry, be happy.

Everything will work out in the end.

You have so much to be grateful for.

Always look on the bright side.

This constant encouragement of happy and positive emotions is referred to as toxic positivity but can be harmful and hurtful to people who have experienced trauma or depression.

You may read on social media about "Self-Love". Self-Love?! That may feel like an impossible destination for you, making you feel more negatively about yourself. Self-love can seem an unattainable goal for someone who may dislike, or even loathe, themself. "How can I love myself when I don't even like myself?"

You can't flick a switch and love yourself. It takes hard work and is challenging as you must directly face the painful reality of how you think about yourself. You may find it hard when you realise how cruel you have been to yourself for years. This is difficult. Journal about it and seek support.

You may read about "Self-Care". This may leave you cold because you don't value yourself enough to think you deserve self-care. You are at the bottom of the list of people you care about. You might not have even included yourself on the list. You wouldn't even contemplate giving yourself any time for self-care. Everyone else needs you. You must put their needs first. You may think you are not worthy of self-care.

During periods of self-doubt, be mindful of what happened to create these feelings. What caused that self-loathing? The things that happened, the words that were said that left a damaging imprint on your heart.

If you find that some pages on social media cause you pain or anxiety or to doubt yourself, unfollow them. If you don't feel uplifted by them, unfollow them. These are boundaries around your social media usage.

Your mental health is your top priority.

This is hard work, so give yourself those breaks. Permit yourself just to be.

In all this work:

- Do it when it feels right.
- Stop when it doesn't.
- Stop when it feels overwhelming.
- Stop if you are exhausted.

You may find that you feel tired. This can be emotionally exhausting and draining work. Taking rest is vital.

Rest and Relaxation

Schedule time to relax and rest. Give your brain some downtime. Give it time to do things that take your mind off the past – a rest from thinking and processing.

Do things that encourage you to focus on the present, the here and now, and the world around you. Take time to notice and savour. Take time to have some fun if you feel able to.

Start to think about things that help you feel better. Activities that soothe your head and your heart.

Write a list of mindful activities that work for you and build these into your schedule.

Pause regularly and get into the habit of asking yourself what you need. Not what you want, but what you NEED.

The Golden Questions

Regularly ask yourself these Golden Questions from Lori Fitzgerald: The Therapy Den

(https://www.facebook.com/therapydenonline)

Sit down in a quiet space and see what comes up when you ask yourself these questions:

1. "How am I in this moment? (Physically, mentally, emotionally, and energetically)
2. What do I need right now/today? (Not want but need)
3. What's the most meaningful action I can take for myself today.
4. What's the most loving action I can take for myself today."

Cultivate the habit of checking in with yourself and taking action.

The Power of Connection

Humans are wired to connect.

Edward Hallowell, MD, published a book entitled *Connect* in 1999 that discusses the importance of connection. He defines connection as "feeling a part of something larger than yourself, feeling close to another person or group, feeling welcomed and understood."

Hallowell writes: "Just as we need vitamin C each day, we also need a dose of the human moment – positive contact with other people."

My reading and writing lead me to connect with people through social media. For me, this happened simultaneously as the first COVID lockdown started in the UK when connecting virtually was the only option.

I followed the social media pages for the authors of the books I had read and started to find other psychotherapists and trauma specialists who "spoke" to me and my experience. Their posts would make me go, "Yes, that's it". Some would sting or hurt, and I would unfollow those straight away to protect my mental health.

It is worth saying that by this point, I was seeing a psychotherapist weekly, so I was being supported in processing my trauma.

I started to gain the confidence to reach out beyond reading books and following professionals on social media. Some of the professionals I followed on social media ran closed groups on Facebook. It felt safer for me to be within these groups as they had boundaries, and the group had a moderator. I felt more protected.

The problem with responding to posts on Facebook is that people in your circle who are also your Facebook friends may be able to see what you post, and this may not be something you feel ready for yet.

Within a closed group, you can see if anyone you know is in the group. These groups are usually moderated, and people who don't follow the group's rules are removed. Do check the rules and get a flavour for the group. You may be asked to answer some questions before you are permitted to join the group.

Some groups offer the chance to post anonymously.

You may join a group and not get the vibes you hope for. Leave the group. You may feel easily overwhelmed if there are many posts or people are sharing things that trigger you. Always protect your mental health. If it doesn't feel right, it isn't suitable for you at this point. You can always return to it a later date if you wish to.

I joined a private group called Trauma Thrivers, created by Lou Lebentz, a therapist, trauma specialist, Eye Movement Desensitisation and Reprocessing Clinician and transformational speaker. I learned, and continue to learn, so much from this group. Presentations, experiences and ideas are shared on different aspects of healing from trauma.

This group includes many professionals in the trauma field and people at different stages of healing in their trauma experience.

I joined another group that I thought would resonate but chose to come out of it because there were so many members and posts that I became overwhelmed.

Reaching Out

It can feel huge to reach out. This is because it IS huge. This may be the first time you have reached out and acknowledged what happened to you. It could be the first time you have shared anything about your experiences.

It may be that you have isolated yourself from people to protect yourself. If you're not around people, they can't hurt you.

Loneliness in thoughts and experiences can lead us to disconnect from others and society. Disconnecting is a form of protection, but it is ultimately damaging.

Disconnecting to protect ourselves makes connecting with others harder, so always be gentle with yourself. How can you connect when you have started to cut yourself off? An online connection can seem more manageable. You don't need to establish a relationship with the people you are interacting with. You don't have to see them in person, and you don't have to be friends with them.

Beware of how you respond to others' reactions to your posts. Start small. Don't overshare. Get a flavour for the group first by observing posts and comments and see if it's a good fit for you. Don't feel you have to rush in and share a lot.

The ultimate aim of social media is to connect with people.

Sharing can create a connection with others and safe connection is important for all aspects of our health.

.

"When we establish human connections within the context of shared experience, we create community wherever we go."

Gina Greenlee,
Postcards and Pearls: Life Lessons from Solo Moments on the Road

Eight Tips for Reaching Out and Connecting on Social Media

1. Look at social media pages and private Facebook groups that resonate with your experience.
2. Read the rules of the group.
3. Be in the group for a while – observe the group and connect with how it makes you feel.
4. If you feel anxious about connecting, practise writing a reply to a post.
5. If you feel confident, post a message or question in the group.
6. Unfollow any pages or groups that leave you feeling uncomfortable.
7. Always protect your emotional and mental health and treat yourself with kindness and compassion – journal what comes up to help you process what is coming up for you.
8. Ask yourself the Golden Questions regularly.

CHAPTER FOUR
Starting with a Whisper

When you feel ready to speak to someone about what happened to you, you only need one person to start with. One person to metaphorically take your hand and say, "You can do this", or "I'm here for you." They don't have to say these words aloud. It's more a feeling you get from them – that speaking up is okay. It's okay to say whatever you want to say. It's okay to speak your truth.

Talking aloud helps us make sense of the things that happened to us. It allows us to move it out of our minds and changes how our trauma feels to us. Your thoughts and memories could be chaotic, and you may not know what you want to say first, so take your time and consider what you want to share when you open up.

"The longer someone tucks away trauma, the harder it is for them to speak about it"

Shari Botwin,
Thriving After Trauma – Stories of Living and Healing

Don't diminish how hard it is to find your voice and speak your truth. It takes strength and courage to speak up.

In the past, you may have felt that you had to stay quiet about what happened to you. You may have thought it was wrong to speak up, or that pretending things hadn't happened was the best thing to do. You may have felt that you should never speak up as you would be told your memories of the trauma were wrong; you would somehow betray your family by speaking up.

But you can't shake those memories, however hard you try, nor can you understand them. They cause you inner turmoil. Your mind keeps returning to them, and you cannot dismiss them. It may start to feel like there is no other option than to face them head-on.

It may feel like you want and need someone to talk to. Someone you can share these experiences with. Someone to listen to you. Someone to believe what you are saying. Someone to validate you and to tell you it will all be okay.

Start to speak up when you feel ready and to the person you feel most comfortable and emotionally safe sharing with. This might be someone in your circle, or it might be a professional therapist or counsellor.

Self-Invalidation

Here are some statements that you may have said to yourself when the memories have come up before:

"It wasn't that bad."

"It could be worse."

"What I am going through is nothing compared to......."

"I need to wear my big girl pants and move on."

"It happened a long time ago. I should be over it by now."

"I shouldn't feel this way. I have so much to be grateful for."

"Maybe I'm overreacting."

Each of these statements invalidates your feelings and you. You are telling yourself that it is wrong to feel the way you do. You are denying yourself the chance to feel and process what is coming up for you. You are denying what happened to you and its impact on you. You are denying how you felt during those experiences. You are pushing important feelings to one side and ignoring them. You are ignoring what your mind and body are trying to tell you.

By definition, invalidation is rejecting, dismissing or minimising someone's feelings. It implies that a person's experience is not important, wrong, or unacceptable.

Self-invalidation is doing this to yourself.

Next time you notice yourself doing this (you may notice that "I should...." is often at the beginning of a self-invalidating statement), try to be more patient, understanding and empathetic with yourself.

It's okay to feel like this.

Remind yourself, "What I am going through is valid. My feelings and my needs are important.

I need some time to let myself process how I am feeling. I can feel something isn't right, so I need to allow myself to feel what I feel."

Try saying these statements to yourself:

I hear you.
I see you.
It's okay to feel this way.
I get it.

You may have invalidated your memories and experiences for years. Telling yourself things weren't that bad. Trying to stuff those bad memories back down in the hope they would go away. But they are not going away. In fact, they are intensifying.

Talking to someone may be the next step – just one person.

Start with a whisper, with however much of the story you feel prepared to talk about and take it gently.

Once you start feeling that you have the confidence to speak up to someone in your circle, you may have additional worries. "What if the person doesn't believe me?" "What if they dismiss what I tell them?" You can be pushed further into shame if someone else invalidates your memories and experiences. "They said it wasn't that bad, so I must be exaggerating. I must be wrong." You start to internalise your thoughts again, and the self-invalidation intensifies.

This further diminishes your experience and could shut you down.

The Power of Language

Language has both the power to harm and the power to heal.

The language you use when listening to someone's experience makes a real difference.

Your language can make someone feel seen and heard.

Your language can make someone feel supported and cared for.

Your language can also make someone feel diminished.

Your language can invalidate someone.

Your language can shut someone down.

Invalidation

"That happened a long time ago."

"Oh, I'm sure they didn't mean it."

"You're not the only one."

"But, you are so lucky that....."

"No family is perfect."

"I don't know anyone who doesn't have issues with their family."

"Do you think it might just be a generational thing?"

"I think we're all a bit like that."

"But they're your family."

These are all examples of invalidation.

Invalidation is disrespectful.

Invalidation hurts.

Invalidation can be sugar coating the person's reality by trying to put a positive spin on it.

A positive attitude in these situations can silence authentic emotions, which is unhelpful.

The invalidated person may leave the conversation feeling confused and full of self-doubt. They could feel anger. They could feel disappointment. They could feel sadness. They could feel misunderstood.

No matter how or why it happens, invalidation can create confusion and distrust. The person may decide not to open up again. They may be guarded as to what they share with you in the future.

Most people make comments like these unintentionally. They could be trying to cheer the person up in a stressful situation or trying to soften the emotional blow of what the person is sharing. But even though this type of emotional invalidation is done by accident and has well-meaning intentions, it doesn't make it hurt any less.

Well-intentioned advice can do a lot of damage.

"Beware, your advice can hurt and can potentially do serious harm. Better not to give any directions at all if you aren't sure. Understanding, patience and sympathy are in any case way more valuable commodities than even well-informed advice."

Dr Tim Cantopher,
Depressive Illness, The Curse of the Strong.

Advice for Preparing to Speak Up for the First Time

Now you know about invalidation and how potentially damaging it can be, there are steps you can take to help you prepare for speaking up.

If I knew then what I know now, there would have been an initial conversation before sharing anything. This could have prevented any invalidation or comments that stung me. I had some rather wounding conversations that took my healing significantly backwards.

I hope the advice I share helps you to speak up, and I hope it enables you to get a reaction that will support rather than hinder your healing. Someone not reacting the way you need can be very harmful and can take you further into a negative spiral.

As Kathryn Mannix writes in *Listen, How to Find the Words for Tender Conversations*, "The way the listener behaves is crucial to opening up or closing down the safety of the connection."

I write what I have learned in the form of a letter. I am not suggesting you use this letter or send it as an email, but you can if you wish. You may prefer an initial conversation where you can set these boundaries before sharing happens.

Dear (friend),

I want to share some information with you about my past. It is sensitive information, and it is not easy for me to speak about it. It feels very tender, and I want to ensure that speaking up doesn't hurt me further.

First, I want to check that you have the headspace to listen to such sensitive information at this point. I don't want to put you in a difficult position or overwhelm you.

Please let me know if you can listen to me at this time. I fully understand if not.

Thank you

You may feel hurt if they say they cannot have this conversation with you, but this could be because of things in their life that you don't know about.

Saying they can't listen is better than having them listen and invalidating you because they have too much of their own to cope with.

If the person states that they can listen to you, setting some parameters and boundaries around the conversation is essential.

Dear (friend),

Thank you for agreeing to listen to me.

Before I talk to you, I want to set some boundaries to protect us during this tender conversation.

I ask that you listen to me without feeling you have to say anything.

I may get agitated. Allow me to feel any pain that comes up when I speak.

I don't want you to feel any responsibility that you need to take on any of my pain.

I don't want advice or your opinion on what I am telling you. I want to share it with you. Speaking aloud will help me process and it is part of my ongoing healing.

Please don't suggest ways that you think you can fix it. You can't.

Please don't judge or minimise anything I say.

Please don't try to justify any of the actions of the people I tell you about. Doing this would leave me feeling diminished or abandoned and be painful.

Please sit with me and support me in finding my way through this. I know you want the best for me and want me to be okay, but I need to deal with it in my own way and at my own pace.

You can't make it better for me, but you can hold the space for me, and I will be genuinely grateful for that.

Thank you

You may feel uncomfortable telling someone how to be with you when they have kindly agreed to be part of this conversation, but it is for your emotional safety and protection and for theirs too.

The experience of your initial sharing within your circle will influence future sharing and your healing, so doing this preparatory work, although it may be uncomfortable, is essential.

"We unwrap our sorrow like an onion. How people respond to the outer layers inform us as to how much deeper we can go."

Kathryn Mannix,
Listen – How to Find the Words for Tender Conversations

So, start with a whisper.

Think carefully about who you would like to speak to and set those boundaries beforehand.

Speak up to one person to start with. See how it feels. There is no rush. Be gentle with yourself before, during and after the conversation.

After the conversation, you may feel emotionally and physically exhausted, so schedule time to rest. Offer yourself compassionate touch and allow yourself to feel the emotions that come up. You can journal about it.

It is incredibly powerful if you speak up and feel heard, seen and believed. I found it intensely emotional, and it felt like such a breakthrough after years of being told my memories and feelings were wrong.

"Trauma is personal. It does not disappear if it is not validated. When it is ignored or invalidated the silent screams continue internally heard only by the one held captive. When someone enters the pain and hears the screams healing can begin."

Danielle Bernock,
Emerging with Wings: A True Story of Lies,
Pain, And the LOVE that Heals

Once you have had the experience of speaking up with one person, you may decide you wish to speak up more to that person or someone else. This may be the point at which you feel ready to seek one-to-one professional help.

It may be too soon for professional help. You might prefer a group setting. See if there are face-to-face peer support groups in your area or online groups if you prefer to do this work virtually. Speaking within a group of people who understand your situation can be very powerful. But there is no rush, and as I say again and again throughout this book, there is no time frame for this work.

When I was most vulnerable, I first spoke up to a close friend. I felt safe with her, but I only told her a small amount of information. Starting to speak up was a big deal for me, so I took it gently. I dipped my toes in. I tested the waters. I whispered gently.

A comfortable way to share with a friend who lives far away was to record audio messages and send them to her. I didn't tell her too much in one go. Some memories I wanted to share, some I didn't. It would have been too overwhelming for her if I had told her lots of things at once, and it would have been exhausting for me.

Memories were coming up all the time and at different stages. Once I had processed some memories, others would come up, almost shouting, "My turn now, you need to deal with me now".

The beauty of voice messages is that there is no direct interaction. This felt safer for me. When I felt emotionally ready, I could listen to her messages, her reaction, and her supportive words. Also, she could take her time to absorb what I was telling her and think about how she wanted to respond. In a face-to-face conversation, the listener doesn't have that chance. These memories are hard for you, but they can also be hard for someone else to hear about.

This is HARD work. Acknowledge your strength and your bravery but do begin to whisper.

Tell your story.
Shout it. Write it.
Whisper it if you have to.
But tell it.
Some won't understand it.
Some will outright reject it.
But many will thank you for it.
And then the most magical
thing will happen.
One by one, voices will start
whispering, 'Me, too.'
And your tribe will gather.
And you will never feel alone
again."

L.R. Knost
Shared by @Ravenous Butterflies on Facebook

Eight Tips for Reaching Out and Connecting on Social Media

1. Look at social media pages and closed Facebook groups that resonate with your experience.
2. Read the rules of the group.
3. Be in the group for a while – observe the group and connect with how it makes you feel.
4. If you feel anxious about connecting, practise writing a reply to a post.
5. If you feel confident, post a message or question in the group.
6. Unfollow any pages or groups that leave you feeling uncomfortable.
7. Always protect your emotional and mental health and treat yourself with kindness and compassion – journal to help you process what is coming up for you.
8. Ask yourself the Golden Questions regularly. (See Chapter 3)

CHAPTER FIVE

Connecting with "Your" People

"We humans are social beings. We come into the world as the result of others' actions. We survive here in dependence on others. Whether we like it or not, there is hardly a moment of our lives when we do not benefit from others' activities. For this reason, it is hardly surprising that most of our happiness arises in the context of our relationships with others."

The Dalai Lama

Connection with others can bring so much to our lives, but connecting can feel challenging, if not impossible, when you are struggling.

Anxiety, depression or trauma can cause you to close in on yourself, stay at home as much as possible and cut yourself off from everything and everyone to protect yourself.

You may not feel well enough to be around people, even your best friends, or even to stay in touch. Sometimes getting through the day is enough. You may not have the words to explain what is going on for you. That requires energy, and you may not have any.

You may be unable to talk about how you feel because that might meet with judgement.

Reducing contact with people or cutting yourself off entirely may feel safer.

Be gentle and compassionate with yourself if this is your reality. Sometimes you need time to be, and being on your own for a while allows this.

But when you do feel ready to connect, it's important to connect with the right people, who will support your emotional health and wellness. Your people.

Are You Connecting with Your People?

You may never have given much attention to the people you spend time with. You may never have thought about the effect the people you connect with have on you.

"You are the average of the five people you spend the most time with."

Jim Rohn

If this is the case, are you spending time with five people you want to be like?

This may sound like a silly question to some, but to those affected by trauma, you may be trauma bonded to family members and other people out of a sense of duty or due to a sense of familiarity without realising it.

There may be people in your life who cause you emotional harm. There may be people you feel you must maintain a relationship with because they are part of your family or people you have been friends with for a while and so you feel compelled to keep them in your life.

This chapter will discuss how you can start considering who your people are. First, let's think about two categories of people from an energetic perspective: drains and radiators.

Drains

Drains suck the energy and power out of you. After spending time with them, you feel tired and think more negatively about yourself and the world. You may find that you don't look forward to seeing these people and that you are anxious about being in their company.

Drains tend to be negative, moan, and judge or belittle other people.

A relationship with a drain can be toxic/dysfunctional.

Radiators

Radiators are the opposite. Time spent with them is a joy, and it feels like time goes quickly. Radiators exude positivity and warmth, and time spent with them leaves you feeling happy, energised and optimistic. They tend to be good listeners and have a positive outlook on life.

The radiators are your people. Radiators are happy for your success. They uplift you, support you and can be with you during the dark and the happy times.

Becoming aware of who the drains and radiators are in your life has an enormous effect on your wellbeing. However, this is not always easy to process when the drains are people you feel you cannot avoid for various reasons.

In my case, I had many justifiable reasons why I was distancing myself from people. I was in utter denial about the impact that they were having on me. But looking back, I was cutting myself off from most people to protect myself. If I wasn't around people, they couldn't hurt me, and I was REALLY hurting.

Once I started to feel better and ready to connect again, I began to connect with how I felt both within my mind and in my body when I was with different people.

I asked myself some questions to see how I was feeling mentally and physically:

1. **At the thought of meeting up with them**
   - Was I anxious?
   - Why was I anxious?
   - Did I want to meet up with them, or was I doing it because I felt I had to?
   - Why was I meeting up with them if I didn't want to?

2. **When I was with them**

   - How did I feel in my mind during my time with them?
   - How did I feel in my body when I met with them?
   - Was I fully present with them?
   - Did I feel comfortable in their presence?
   - Was I in the moment, or was I in my head, thinking and worrying?
   - Was I worried about what to say, or did I feel open and relaxed?
   - Did I fear judgement or criticism?

3.   Afterwards

- Did I feel good about myself?
- Did they leave me wanting to see them again, or was I relieved and glad it was over?
- How did my body feel? Was I tired or drained?

Connecting within and asking myself these questions helped me to see who was good for my emotional and mental health and who I wanted to spend time with, rather than feeling a duty to be with them.

I started to ask myself why I was spending so much time around people who left me feeling low and anxious. Once I connected with my feelings, I could sense the life force leaving me when I was around them.

If you have experienced trauma during your childhood, you may have been drawn to people during childhood and your adulthood who felt familiar. You may have some wonderful friends, but you may also have been attracted to people who have traits of your family. People who treat you like your family did. Start to take notice of this and be compassionate with yourself.

It can feel painful when you realise that someone you had considered a good friend has treated you in harmful ways or has taken advantage of your giving nature. You might criticise yourself for accepting it.

Be aware that this is a behaviour you were used to. If you weren't taught your value as a child, and were treated poorly, you might have accepted unacceptable behaviour from others.

As Maya Angelou says,

"Forgive yourself for not knowing what you didn't know before you learned it."

Knowing Who Your People Are

How do you know who "your people" are?

It isn't necessarily that you are alike or have the same interests; it is a feeling, an energy.

Here are some questions you can consider:

- Do you look forward to being in their company?
- Does life feel joyous when you are with them?
- Do you feel joyful when you are around them?
- Do you feel accepted, acknowledged, and visible with them?
- Do they understand when you don't get back to them?
- Do they check in with you when you are unwell or haven't been in touch for a while?
- Do they listen to you with empathy?
- Do they judge and criticise you and your choices?
- Do they belittle you?
- Are they open and honest with you?
- Do you feel like the best version of yourself when you are with them?
- Can you be fully yourself with them?
- Are they happy for you when things are going well, or do they seem to prefer it when you are struggling?
- Are they competitive with you?

"Across my research, I define connection as the energy that exists between people when they feel seen, heard and valued; when they can give and receive without judgment; and when they derive sustenance and strength from the relationship."

Brene Brown – *Atlas of the Heart Mapping, Meaningful Connection and the Language of Human Experience.*

You need and deserve genuine connection – people suitable for your emotional and mental health.

Friendships

We meet many people on our journey through life. Friends come into our lives through a shared life experience, e.g., school, university, work, having children, shared relationships etc.

Some friends come into our lives, and we have a close bond, but when that connection ends, e.g., you leave a workplace, the friendship can fade too.

Some friendships last a lifetime.

Some run their natural course.

Think about your friends. You may have lots of friends, or you may have a few friends. The number doesn't matter. The quality of the friendship and the effect of the friendship on you are the most critical factors.

Knowing someone for years does not necessarily make them a better friend.

If you discover that someone you had considered a friend isn't emotionally healthy for you, you have every right to let go of them and remove yourself from painful situations. Some people simply aren't right for us anymore.

If it feels too scary to let someone go, limit your contact with them. Your friendship may not end, and you may not want it to, but it can and needs to change. You deserve healthy friendships.

What you are going through may be changing you as a person. You are starting to speak up and to protect yourself. Some friends may struggle with that. They only know the old you. Some will celebrate your new strength; some may want you to be the person you used to be.

"We have three types of friends in life: Friends for a reason, friends for a season, and friends for a lifetime."

Z.K. Abdelnour

Friendships change and evolve; some end. This is natural, but it is not something that is often discussed.

A friendship ending is the end of that person's part in your life. I don't want to diminish how painful this can be. Allow yourself time to grieve and process all the emotions that come up.

But don't make yourself ill for someone else.

Don't break yourself for anyone. Don't allow someone to treat you like your family did because that treatment feels familiar.

Your wellbeing, health and your emotional safety are your number one priority.

"Sometimes it is not enough just to have respect for yourself. Sometimes you have to actively protect yourself from people and situations that would drain your energies or hurt your feelings. Looking out for yourself is a primary responsibility, whether it's setting boundaries or making sure that others aren't allowed to limit your life."

Lindsay C Gibson, PsyD,
Self-Care for Adult Children of Emotionally Immature Parents

You may not have ever felt this before, but you are in control of who you give your time and energy to. This thought could fill you with anxiety and fear. Be kind and compassionate. You don't need to do anything straight away. Take your time and do what feels right for you, but put yourself and your needs first.

You matter and you deserve to be in friendships and relationships that light up your world.

There are people out there who you don't know yet but will become new friends when you feel ready to start connecting again. This is an exciting thought, but it may scare you too – take one step at a time and move at your pace.

Some of my friendships have changed during my ongoing trauma healing.

Some people couldn't or didn't want to hear my pain, and I get that. People have lots going on in their lives that we may not be aware of, plus the world was coming to grips with the Coronavirus pandemic for much of the time I was going through this.

Some friends wanted me to be well, and I understand that too. Sadly, trauma healing is not like this. Trauma healing comes in waves. It can feel very dark at times. It can feel like you are trudging through treacle. You can feel hopeless and helpless, and that life will never get better. You can meander from being well to unwell, with lots of feelings in between. This can be hard for friends to understand.

Triggers are always there. Triggers can hit you like a punch in the stomach, leaving you feeling winded and bruised. It can feel like your triggers are slowing down your healing. This affects your health and how you show up for friends. They may struggle with this.

After my breakdown, I knew instinctively that I needed to connect with new people and do activities just for me. I had cut myself off from most people when I was ill during my 40s. Some of this was because I was mixing with people that weren't for me, and the times we spent together didn't bring me joy. I also had some lovely friends, but I didn't have the energy to spend much time with them. I felt mentally exhausted.

Something deep inside told me I had to do something about it, that I needed to connect with my people. I knew that I had to start paying close attention to who I gave my energy to.

I had spent most of my life trying to get love, acknowledgement and attention from a few people – primarily family members - but was encouraged by my therapist to turn around and notice the other people in my life. Other people who like and love me for who I am.

I joined a choir, and a connection there led me to attend a women's circle, making new connections along the way. Everyone I met at the different activities played a part in my healing, but few knew my reality, which was a relief.

I could enjoy the activities without talking about my health. I wasn't ashamed of my reality, but it was fantastic to talk about other things and enjoy life again without the constant dark cloud.

After a few months, I started going to Tai Chi sessions. Meditation didn't work for me as my brain was full, heavy and painful, but Tai Chi, with its flowing movements and Yoga Nidra, worked like a dream for me.

After years of not doing anything for myself, I was doing things just for me, and it felt good. I started to feel alive again. I began to feel like I was human again.

I didn't put myself under any pressure to make friends, which helped. I was there to connect, not to make friends. If a connection became a friend, that was a bonus.

As my confidence started to build, I reached out and joined online communities and decided to take an online coaching course.

There were three of us taking the course, and we had the most profound connection. They helped me get through the toughest of times and were incredible cheerleaders and companions along the way.

Speaking up has also brought old friends back into my life, some of whom I had not been directly in touch with for many years. They reached out and offered me incredible support.

Without a shadow of a doubt, everyone that came into my life during these times, whether I am still connected with them or not, has left a legacy in my healing, and I am grateful for that.

They have given me a renewed zest for life and renewed hope.

Connection has wonderful ripple effects in your life.

Connection leads to further connection, and I have made some incredible new friends and contacts since my breakdown.

People who are good for me, uplift me, bring joy into my world and people with whom I am seen and heard.

My people.

"When you're with good people, the sun always shines."

Miriam Margolyes,
This Much is True

IT'S NOT JUST YOU • 73

Six Tips for Connecting with Your People

1. Start to think about how you feel when you are around people.
2. Evaluate your energy levels, confidence and emotions before, during and after you spend time with people.
3. Remember that you matter and how you feel in a friendship is the most important thing. Limit your time, or don't spend time with people who make you feel bad about yourself, especially when you are feeling low.
4. Start to connect with new people when it feels right for you.
5. Don't put pressure on yourself to make friends; enjoy connecting.
6. Schedule time to see different people within your tribe when you feel well enough – you will feel better for it.

CHAPTER SIX
Seeking Professional Help

It may be hard for you to accept that you need additional help, that you can't get through this on your own, or with the support of your people.

If this is you, I hear you.

You may have been given the message within your family that things that happened should not be discussed.

You may have been sent the message that getting help is a weakness, maybe even an indulgence.

But getting help is important.

You deserve to be heard and supported by someone who understands the dynamics within an emotionally dysfunctional family and who understands trauma.

You may feel vulnerable or fragile. This is entirely understandable.

You may have kept quiet about things that happened for a long time.

You may have been trying to make sense of your past for a long time.

You may have thought that ploughing on and coping would be the best way. But that hasn't worked. You feel overwhelmed.

You don't need to rush into getting help but start to take action when it feels right.

There are different avenues you can explore.

Educate yourself. Read, research and see what feels right for you.

A first start could be speaking to your doctor to see what options they can offer. You can seek a second opinion or talk to other professionals if you are not happy with the options or if you do not feel comfortable.

If you don't feel ready to speak with someone face-to-face, message them. Establish initial contact in the right way for you. Your emotional safety is paramount. It can feel scary to begin to talk with someone you don't know. You might be worried about what else will come up once you start to talk. It might feel like once you turn on the tap you won't be able to turn it off again.

I would advise you to write some notes before the appointment, so you feel prepared. You may find that you get anxious during the appointment and forget to say important things. Your notes will help.

From my personal experience, working with a professional helps you lighten the emotional load.

A professional who isn't directly involved in your life.

A professional relationship with boundaries and emotional safety.

A professional who understands that lack of emotional attachment in childhood is trauma.

A professional in the trauma world who understands the complex nature of trauma healing and can hold space for you.

When I had my breakdown I was given medication.

I took sleeping tablets for one week and slept for most of that week. I hadn't slept well for years, waking up at 3 am most days with thoughts and traumatic memories flying around my head. Not only was I sleeping poorly, but my mind was always active, which was exhausting.

I was also prescribed a low-dose antidepressant.

I had spent years taking painkillers, having hospital appointments, and appointments with the doctor to deal with the variety of physical pains I experienced. The medication stopped the physical pain momentarily, but it wasn't going away for longer than a few hours.

Over the years, I experienced daily headaches, migraines, horrendous period pain, gastric issues, pelvic pain, and shoulder and neck pain. I was ill daily. I didn't know what it felt like to be physically well. I also didn't know what it felt like to have a clear head. A mind that wasn't always in overdrive.

I now know that it was stuck trauma in my body. I had no idea back then.

I am a Compassionate Coach and mentor. I am not an expert in the trauma field, but I am training to be a trauma-informed coach.

I have complex post-traumatic stress disorder (CPTSD) and have been on a healing journey for a few years. Discovering that I have CPTSD gave me such a sense of release and relief as for the first time I saw the connection between my mental and physical ill health. The connection between my mind and my body.

I have survived trauma and am now thriving. I have inner freedom, harmony, self-acceptance and self-compassion in my life.

In this chapter, I will share the healing work I did with professionals, with brief definitions from experts.

This is my personal experience.

I am not suggesting that what worked for me will work for you.

We are all different. Our experiences are different. Our trauma and how it affects us are different.

I hope my experience will give you hope that there is a way through what you are feeling. Also, the knowledge that you can live and flourish after trauma.

There are other treatments for trauma that I did not access, for example, Eye Movement Desensitisation and Reprocessing (EMDR). I won't write about them as I have no personal experience, but if you are interested, you can do some research online to find out more.

What is Post-Traumatic Stress Disorder (PTSD) and Complex PTSD (CPTSD)?

Mily Gomez states that "PTSD often describes a single event that we associate with accidents, traumatic medical procedures, accidents, and violence. In recent years there has been increasing recognition of the psychological impact of prolonged, recurrent, and interpersonal trauma in childhood. This type of trauma has been termed Complex PTSD (CPTSD).

The evidence suggests that most complex trauma originates in childhood. The prolonged trauma experienced may have fundamentally altered the individual's personality. Therefore, CPTSD combines elements of PTSD and personality disorders.

One big threatening and distressful event (1 cup at once) can distress you just as much as less distressful and non-life-threatening events (many T-spoons that make 1 cup). In the end, the cup got full by either one single life-threatening event or recurring distressful non-life-threatening events.

People minimize their experiences because they compare them to a single horrific event. Trauma is not in the event but in the aftermath. Trauma is in the nervous systems of a full cup.

Your reactions, thoughts, and adaptations make sense when you see that the cup is full. "

@latibulecounseling on Instagram

My cup overflowed dramatically. I didn't know about the connection between my mental and physical health. I didn't know that trauma from childhood impacted me physically.

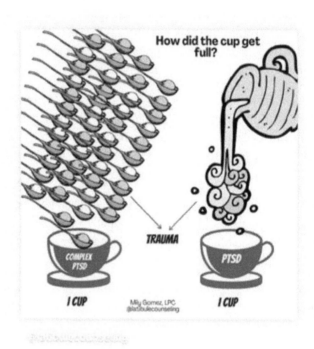

Diagram 1 – Mily Gomez, LPC
@latibulecounseling on Instagram

What are the Three Stages of Trauma Healing?

Diagram 2 -
https://www.instagram.com/traumathrivers_loulebentz

Lou Lebentz states that "There are three stages to trauma healing that need to be followed so that the process can happen effectively without re-traumatisation at any point. It's also why it has to occur sequentially with someone who understands the stages needed to metabolise trauma within someone's system and body in a safe way.

If trauma healing happens too quickly, the person can become flooded or destabilised, which is almost like turning a tap on too quickly into someone's system when they've not used water for a while. Going from dehydrated to hydrated has to happen drop by drop.

A system that's not used to being fully connected via mind, body, and emotions needs to open the faucets slowly so the person can adjust to the flow of sensations in the body again. Some people I work with have not been connected to their bodies or systems for years and have not been able to feel for a very long time. It's too scary to go straight into the water until you've learnt how to dip your toe in, your leg in, and then doggy paddle in the shallow end for a bit.

Excuse the analogies, but I think they are helpful when working with systems that have essentially shut off. Some people are not connected to themselves or any other systems, so it needs to be a slow, organic process until one of them feels safe enough at each mini step to widen their ability to tolerate sensations and emotions in the body."

Lou Lebentz at
https://www.instagram.com/traumathrivers_loulebentz

This quote and diagram clearly illustrate that trauma healing takes time and that you need support from someone who understands these stages.

There is no quick fix to healing from trauma.

I will never downplay how hard it is. But the time and the effort required are worth it.

What is Psychotherapy?

"Psychotherapy can be a powerful, life-changing experience which can help you to improve your mental health, overcome social or emotional challenges, and fulfil your potential. A trained psychotherapist can support you to:

- express your feelings and process them in a safe and supportive relationship
- gain deeper insight into the issues you face
- talk about things in a confidential environment that you might not feel be able to discuss with anyone else
- find better ways to cope with feelings and fears
- change the way you think and behave to improve your mental and emotional wellbeing
- improve relationships in your life, including with yourself
- make sense of any clinical diagnoses you have had by understanding what has happened to you
- heal from trauma
- learn to communicate better and tolerate differences in yourself and others."

https://www.psychotherapy.org.uk/seeking-therapy/what-is-psychotherapy/

A few months after my breakdown, I started talking to a psychotherapist weekly. I chose one who is person-centred.

I decided that I could not wait for a referral under the Health Service in England and opted for private psychotherapy. I researched online, started following local psychotherapists on social media and asked for recommendations.

I had a free, no-obligation chat before committing to doing any work. This is crucial. If you have a choice as to who you will work with, chat with different therapists, and ask any questions you have.

Connect with how you feel during and after the initial conversation, and then take some time before deciding who you want to work with. This is close, sensitive and painful work. You might be talking about things you have never discussed with anyone before, so rapport and a feeling of emotional safety are vital for you.

I had previously had therapy at two other times of my life – in my early 20s and again during my mid-40s. Both helped in different ways, but they were not the breakthrough I needed at the time.

After my breakdown, when I was 48 years old, it was the right time. Many memories were coming up back repeatedly. I couldn't live with them in my mind any longer. I needed professional support to help me make sense of things that happened within my family.

I chose a therapist I had an instant rapport with.

I had in-person therapy until the COVID lockdowns started and now have online therapy.

In-person therapy was what I wanted and needed when I started treatment, and I am grateful that I could have face-to-face therapy during my darkest times. Most times, I would come out of the therapy room feeling lighter. I wasn't working at the time due to my health and appreciated being out of the house, taking the chance to travel by train and to go for a coffee afterwards.

Walking to and from the train station gave me the space to breathe and calm down after the session.

Some may prefer online therapy. I wanted and needed to be out of the house and have time before and after the session on my own. This may not be possible at home if you have children or other people/pets who may want your attention as soon as the session finishes.

However, being at home whilst you have therapy, may feel safer for you.

Allow yourself time after the session to sit and be. You could hug yourself or sit with a snuggly blanket as you bring yourself back to the present moment. You are amazing.

Occasionally I found the therapy overwhelming, but I always knew it was what I needed to do if I was going to feel better.

Therapy helped me make sense of the experiences I had replayed in my mind for years. I wasn't asked to re-live the events. This had happened in previous therapy, and it didn't work for me.

My work with my psychotherapist, has changed my health, my outlook and my world in every way. I was expertly guided through the many layers of my trauma. I now know my value and live life in colour after years of merely existing from day to day.

After my breakdown, I started to take a holistic approach to my health. This considers the whole of me, not one illness in isolation. Trauma affects the body, so holistic support is hugely important. You could do some research on holistic practitioners and homeopaths.

What is Homeopathy?

"Homeopathy is a system of complementary medicine that has been used around the world for over 200 years. According to the World Health Organisation it is currently the second most popular form of medicine with an estimated 200 million people using homeopathy on a regular basis.

The aim of homeopathy is to treat the individual, so homeopathic remedies are selected based on a person's specific symptoms and what makes them feel better or worse rather than being given based on a disease label. The remedies are chosen based on the principle of 'like treats like' where a substance that can cause symptoms in large doses can also help to alleviate symptoms when given in very small doses."

Abi Briant-Smith, https://www.facebook.com/HomeopathAbi/

Working with a homeopath – my homeopath is also a mind-body therapist - allowed me to see the close link between my mental and physical health, between the mind and the body. Before this, I had no idea that emotional trauma caused my many years of physical illness.

Working with my homeopath has been incredible. She has got to know my entire health picture, from mental and physical health to what is bothering me, how I am feeling, my sleep and dreams.

I suffered headaches and migraines for years.

I had internal examinations for pelvic pain. So many hospital appointments. I had a laparoscopy. I took painkillers – lots of painkillers over the years. I wanted the pain to go away. I wanted to be able to go for a walk without pain.

After several years of examinations, the doctor concluded it was "undiagnosed pelvic pain."

Working with an osteopath eased the physical pain and working with a homeopath connected my physical and mental pain.

I had neck and shoulder pain for years. I woke up in a lot of pain. Stabbing pains in my shoulder, awful back pain, headaches, and jaw ache. Little did I know that it was trauma.

As I got closer to my breakdown, my health worsened. I got infections that would take a month to clear. I had digestive issues. I developed acute anxiety and depression.

All because of what happened to me and the resulting trauma stuck in my body. Working holistically with my homeopath allowed me to understand this.

I am now so much better. I don't get many headaches and at the time of writing haven't had a migraine in over six months. The pelvic pain, neck and shoulder pains have gone too. If I get pain, I sit with the pain and allow it instead of reaching for the painkillers. I don't fight the pain or rush to get rid of it like I used to.

I am so grateful to my homeopath for my good health.

What is Reiki?

"Reiki (ray-key) is Japanese for 'universal life energy', a term used to describe a system of natural healing. This healing tradition was founded by Dr Mikao Usui in the early 20th century and evolved as a result of his research, experience and dedication.

We live in a world of energy that nourishes and maintains all living things. When this energy flows uninterrupted there is balance and harmony within and around us and we experience a sense of wellbeing. There are many variations of Reiki, but in essence Reiki works at bringing us into balance and is believed therefore to reinforce the body's natural ability to heal itself at all levels, whether physical, mental, emotional or spiritual. It is a tradition that is open to any belief system.

Reiki is a healing process that anyone can benefit from in the normal course of their life. Research using animals and even bacteria suggests it has the ability to reverse stress-induced conditions. It should not, however, be regarded as a cure for conditions. As a natural form of healing Reiki can support and enhance other forms of treatment."

https://www.reikicouncil.org.uk/What-is-Reiki.php

I was lucky enough to connect with someone through a coaching course who was training to become a Reiki Healer.

Our work together was done virtually – yes, virtually! – during the COVID lockdowns.

The physical sensations I felt during the sessions were incredible, and I felt much better after each session. It helped release my physical pain, my stuck energy and gave me a sense of calm and flow in my body. I don't think I had ever felt this before.

What is Shamanic Healing?

"Shamanic healing is about being able to connect with one, or all of the four spirits – 'the four bodies' in a person; the physical, emotional, mental and spiritual.

Healing then requires us to align those bodies with the magnetic energy of source – the creation energy and be able to heal themselves.

This can happen through the use of clearing spirits which don't belong in these bodies – etheric entities for example – or by activating energies within those bodies, or simply having a person look at their dreams.

Shamanic healing can also result in teaching someone how to communicate with spirit. Through shamanic healing, someone – you – can learn to communicate with your body to find out what it's going through and change whatever the body needs.

For example, being able to change the body's temperature or relax certain muscles."

https://shamandurek.com/shamanic/shamanic-healing/

I connected with a Shamanic Healer through a mutual contact. I would never have done shamanic work before; I would have been too cynical about it. But opening my mind has resulted in me trying things that have brought peace and solace to my world.

My shamanic healer is a wonderful person. Our connection is deep and powerful, and I have gained so much from working with her, including a sense of belonging with past generations of my childhood family.

I also connected with an intuitive psychic. The readings with her were nourishing for the mind, body and soul.

What is Emotional Freedom Technique (EFT) Tapping?

"EFT is a practical self-help method that involves using the fingers to gently tap on the body's acupuncture points along the meridian lines of Chinese medicine. It is often referred to as 'EFT Tapping' or simply as 'Tapping'. The therapeutic effects of this technique are recognized around the world. One can use EFT tapping for anxiety, weight loss issues, pain, stress and many other issues.

EFT Tapping helps us tune in to the negative patterns that we form around our uncomfortable thoughts, feelings, or troubling memories. We 'tap' on the correct pressure points while bringing the thoughts or emotions into consciousness. The aim is to find relief, relaxation, and promote healing around the emotional or physical issues that hold us back."

EFT International: https://eftinternational.org/discover-eft-tapping/what-is-eft-tapping/

I found EFT soothing for my mental anguish and physical pain, and it was something I could easily do at home as there are a range of videos on YouTube.

I watched Brad Yates and Julie Schiffman on YouTube, who both have a range of free EFT sessions for different circumstances and emotions.

During my healing, I was introduced to Qigong and Yoga Nidra, both of which are incredibly soothing for my nervous system. They get me out of my head and into my body. They create a sense of ease, flow and peace and I feel wonderful after doing them.

My husband and I spent a lot of money on the different sources of support I accessed. I will never know the full impact of each one in isolation, but the combination of treatments has got me to where I am today so we will never regret it. I am healthier and happier than ever.

It has been a substantial financial investment that we couldn't easily afford. I only worked for nine months during the three years after my breakdown due to health issues. We went from being a two-income household to a single-income family with a child in High School.

But it has been the best investment – an investment in myself that has positively impacted me, my family and all aspects of my life.

If private support is not possible, ask local therapists if they offer any pro bono work.

There may be private Facebook groups that you could join for some support or charities that offer peer support groups online or locally.

You could ask your doctor for information on any services available for you in your local area.

A group I wholeheartedly recommend is Trauma Thrivers on Facebook, run by trauma professional Lou Lebentz. There are many trauma-informed professionals in the group:

https://www.facebook.com/groups/traumathrivers

Whatever form of support you access, I want you to know that you are worthy of help.

You deserve inner peace.

"To all the people who are
working on their healing.
Discovering boundaries.
Learning how to express their
needs.
De-constructing stories.
Re-writing the narrative.
Seeking out inner peace. That
love you are depositing in your
love bank is the best investment
you can make."

@catherine.asta on Instagram

Ten Tips for Reaching Out for Professional Help

1. Talk to your doctor – see what support is available and find out how you access it. Is there a waiting list etc? This will depend on your location.
2. Read and research possible avenues of support.
3. If you are paying privately and can select your support, do your research – what type of support do you want? If you feel overwhelmed with the options, see if there is someone you can contact for advice.
4. Try to get personal recommendations if possible.
5. Make notes about what you want to say when you first approach someone for professional support.
6. Have a chat or correspond with a few practitioners before committing to starting any work.
7. Think about whether you want in-person or virtual appointments. For emotional safety, you may prefer to be at home. Conversely, you might like to be somewhere else, away from people you know.
8. Take your time to decide who you will work with. If someone pressures you, they are not the person to work with. Your needs are of the utmost importance. Do you feel comfortable with the person? How do they make you feel?
9. Open your mind to different sources of support. Try new things if you feel comfortable doing so.
10. Always treat yourself with kindness and compassion.

CHAPTER SEVEN

An Introduction to the Mind-Body Connection and the Nervous System

If someone had told me during my darkest times that I needed to connect more with my body, I would not have had any idea what they were talking about. Looking back, I had lived virtually my whole life in my head – my overthinking, heavy and painful head.

I had utterly disassociated from my body without realising it, but my body was in a lot of pain. I was in mental pain in my head and physical pain in my body, but I didn't know there was a connection between the two. I didn't know anything about the mind-body connection or the link between my physical and mental health.

My body was crying out to me, but I didn't know it and so ploughed on, exhausting myself. I didn't know any other way of being, and I assumed other people also experienced this.

At those darkest times, I was in physical and psychological pain. I struggled to get through each day. It felt like I was dragging myself through the day until I was back in bed that evening.

I started to hate my bedroom as my sleep was so erratic. I woke up at 3 am most days for several years. I associated my bedroom with tossing and turning and memories returning to haunt me. By the time it was 7am and time to get out of bed, I had experienced four hours of painful memories coming back. This was every day. It felt torturous and relentless. I was running on empty.

When you feel ready, you can start to do some reading and research on the mind-body connection. I started to read "The Body Keeps the Score: Brain, Mind and Body in the Healing of Trauma" by Bessel van der Kolk about a year into my breakdown recovery when I felt well enough to read and retain information. I read short sections of the book at a time and made notes. If you have access to this book, I recommend you read Part Five "Paths to Recovery" at this stage.

I needed time away from the book to make notes, process the information and reflect on my past. Be mindful that I was simultaneously working with a professional psychotherapist who could support me in processing what was coming up.

What I know now that I didn't realise then is that:

"Traumatized people chronically feel unsafe inside their bodies: The past is alive in the form of gnawing interior discomfort. Their bodies are constantly bombarded by visceral warning signs, and, in an attempt to control these processes, they often become expert at ignoring their gut feelings and in numbing awareness of what is played out inside. They learn to hide from their selves." Bessel A. van der Kolk, The Body Keeps the Score: Brain, Mind, and Body in the Healing of Trauma

I didn't know that the physical pain I was experiencing was a response to trauma.

I knew nothing of emotional safety. I just knew I experienced stress and anxiety daily and often descended into what I thought were depressive episodes. Some days I could feel a dark cloud descend and was powerless to do anything until it lifted. All I could do was give in to it and rest. I had no physical or mental energy to do anything.

When I saw the doctor, she asked me to write a list of all the symptoms I had experienced leading up to my breakdown and then to refer to that list. She said that if I started to get a number of these symptoms again, it was a message that I needed to take action to protect my health.

Here's the list:

- Migraines
- Neck and shoulder pain – excruciating at times
- Insomnia – waking up at 3 am and not going back to sleep
- Daily headaches
- Erratic and painful menstrual cycle
- Memory loss
- Brain fog
- Getting my words wrong
- Feeling completely blank with what felt like cotton wool going around my head
- Not able to concentrate
- Not able to multi-task
- Low mood
- Anxiety
- Panic attacks
- Shortness of breath when talking

- Sugar cravings and emotional eating
- Thinning nails and hair
- Snappy with my husband and daughter
- Jaw ache
- Cutting myself off from people
- Eyelid twitching
- Frequent colds and infections which antibiotics would not shift
- Feeling overwhelmed
- A loud and busy mind
- Constant negative thoughts
- Feeling worthless
- Forgetfulness
- Pelvic pain
- Digestive issues.

I must add that I also went through perimenopause during these years, so some of the symptoms I experienced may be linked to that stage of life.

Before my breakdown, I sought medical help with a few of the above issues and was given medication which gave some light short-term relief, but nothing more. I had some difficult experiences. I was prescribed addictive medicine for my pelvic pain and had to wean myself off slowly.

I was prescribed daily anti-epilepsy medication to prevent migraines. It didn't get rid of them completely, but it did make me feel like a zombie, so I stopped taking them.

Every time a medication didn't take the pain away, I went further into a negative spiral, thinking I would never feel well again.

No one was connecting the pieces, so, of course, I didn't either.

I wonder why no one that knew me well said it wasn't right that I was ill so regularly. Mind you, I probably wouldn't have listened. One week before my breakdown, my husband commented that I would be signed off if my work didn't do something about my current situation.

I remember wondering what on earth he was talking about. One week later, I broke down. I had been in utter denial.

When the breakdown forced me to stop, my whole life came crashing to a halt, and I got a clear message from myself that I had to do something about it - that only I could do this.

I was raised to think that others were responsible for my happiness and that I was responsible for theirs. I now know that this is not the case. I am responsible for myself, but this was tough to take on board when I was in so much pain, and my energy levels were depleted. At times it felt just like another responsibility and overwhelmed me.

Establishing a Relationship with Your Body

I recommend that you start becoming aware of your body and bodily sensations slowly and steadily. Be mindful of how your body feels and what feels comfortable and uncomfortable for you.

Becoming aware, and establishing a relationship with your body, is a crucial first step before you can befriend your body.

Looking back, I realised I had been awful to my body for years. The voice inside my head told me how horrible my body was, how useless my body was and how my body was failing me regularly.

I wasn't kind to my body when it was in pain. I punished it further. Rather than being a friend to my body, I was its worst enemy. I loathed myself. I loathed my body.

I looked at myself in the mirror and was repulsed by what I saw. I saw nothing but faults and flaws.

It will take time to develop a relationship with your body and appreciate yourself, but it can happen.

Starting to think about how amazing your body is can be an excellent first step.

My body got me through a breakdown. My body gave me my wonderful daughter. My body is stronger and more amazing than I ever realised, but it has taken time for me to reach this level of acceptance and acknowledgement.

You can also become aware of how your body feels when experiencing different emotions. Your body is sending you messages all the time. A good start is to become aware of those messages.

For example, you might feel the following sensations when experiencing joy: warm, tingly, flowing, pulsating, radiating, and expansive.

You might feel the following sensations if you are angry: clenched, hot, pounding head, sweaty hands, tight, shaky, twitchy.

Start to become aware of the signals your body is sending.

How often do you ignore the signals from your body?

Do you listen to your body when it tells you it is hungry, or do you ignore it and suppress those feelings of hunger? Hunger pangs are reminders to eat enough food so you have the energy to get through the day.

Your caregivers may have taught you to only eat at certain times. You may have been told that you had to eat everything on your plate, thus ignoring your body's message that it was full and didn't want or need any more food.

When you explore this, you may get memories of messages you were sent that stopped you from listening to your body and reacting in the way your body wanted you to. Be kind and gentle with yourself; these messages may have left a damaging effect on you. Journalling about it might help.

You may have been told not to cry, get angry, or suppress your emotions. In doing this, you are ignoring your body's needs. You are suppressing yourself, and this causes anguish and illness.

"If you listen to your body when it whispers….you won't have to hear it scream."

Unknown

Listen to Your Body

"It speaks through your energy levels when you feel fatigued or alert.

It speaks through the sensations you feel when you feel restless, heavy, numb or dizzy.

It speaks through your health when you feel aches, pains and tension.

It speaks through your intuition when you have a gut feeling or sense that something is wrong. "

@therapywithabby on Instagram

Start to become aware of the messages your body is sending you.

When you experience a feeling or sensation, explore what is coming up.

What is that feeling trying to tell you?

Is there any action that your body wants you to take?

Start to become more mindful about how you talk about your body within your own mind and others. Are you putting yourself down? Are you saying horrible things about yourself? Be gentle with yourself as you become aware of this. Don't berate yourself. You didn't know any other way.

This relationship will not change overnight when you have spent years disliking or hating your body. Taking small and steady steps that become daily habits can make a huge difference.

When I hear myself say something negative about my body, I have a conversation and change the dynamic to a more positive one. As some people advise, I don't tell my inner critic to go away. Instead, I have a dialogue with my critic and thank her for her opinion but let her know that I disagree. I tell her that I am kinder to myself now, thank you!

This may sound strange, and you may feel awkward doing it initially, but open your mind and try it. See how it feels.

I am now much more appreciative of my body and how it has got me to where I am today – that it has survived the trauma and pain and is mostly well again.

I no longer berate myself if I get ill. I am a friend to my body. I consider what my needs are. Do I need to rest? Do I need to soothe myself? Do I need a hot water bottle? Do I need to go for a walk? Do I need a warm bath, etc?

The Nervous System

"People who've experienced trauma generally develop an oversensitive nervous system and respond to triggers in a heightened way because they're responding from their template, from their history. Trauma survivors are often hypervigilant, always on guard, expecting threats."

Lynne Friedman-Gell, PHD and Joanne Barron PSYD,
Intergenerational Trauma Workbook; Strategies to Support Your Journey of Discovery, Growth and Healing

I will not go into lots of detail about the nervous system as I don't want to overwhelm you.

I offer a brief introduction and invite you to read and research further when you feel ready.

What is the Nervous System?

The body's major controlling, regulatory and communicating system is the nervous system. It is the centre of all mental activity, including thought, learning and memory.

The nervous system is at the heart of our daily experiences.

Understanding how it works is essential in understanding ourselves.

People who have experienced trauma can find it hard to regulate their emotions, especially when triggered by a past traumatic event. If your caregiver could not soothe their own nervous system, you will not have learned how to do this for yourself.

When our nervous system is dysregulated, our emotions can be heightened and overwhelming and can harm our well-being.

You can learn how to attune to your nervous system and use self-soothing strategies that bring you back to a state of inner security and trust, to a place of emotional safety.

Your body tells you if you are in a state of threat.

Your body sends messages that something is wrong, and that action is required.

The nervous system is trying to protect you, but it may be trying to protect you from something from your past rather than what is happening in the present moment.

If you experience a trigger from your past, you can start to reassure your body that you are okay. That you are not in that emotionally unsafe environment now and so do not need protection. Using self-soothing techniques, you can gently and carefully bring yourself back to the present and a feeling of safety.

Doctor Stephen Porges, the author of the Polyvagal Theory, states that there are three different states of nervous system activation:

1. Ventral vagal social engagement

2. Sympathetic activation

3. Dorsal vagal shutdown.

1. The Ventral Vagal State – "I feel connected, I can."

This state is activated when your body perceives safety.

When you are in the ventral state, you are engaged and in the present moment. You feel a sense of peace and a sense of flow. You feel happy and maybe even joyful.

You feel grounded in your body. You feel connected, curious and open. You are mindful of your surroundings and of the people you are with. You feel connected with those people. You feel physically and mentally well.

2. Sympathetic Activation - "I'm in danger, so I must......"

If you start to feel uneasy or unsafe, you go into the nervous system's sympathetic state.

This can be a real danger; a car coming towards you as you cross the road or a perceived threat, or a text from a difficult family member.

When you are in the sympathetic state, you can go into:

Flight

Flight is a feeling of panic, fear, anxiety, and wanting to get away as quickly as possible. It can also include burying yourself in work or exercise.

Fight

Fight can be expressed through rage, anger, irritability or frustration. It can also include high standards, perfectionism or being unfair in personal relationships.

Fawn

Fawning involves people-pleasing. It is brought about by an attempt to avoid conflict. For an adult, this means ignoring your needs and conforming to what you think others want of you.

Those who have experienced trauma may always be wobbling precariously into the sympathetic state, rarely feeling safe or at ease. This is exhausting.

3. The Dorsal Vagal Shutdown – "I can't cope."

If you ignore the signs of the sympathetic state, you go into the dorsal state. This is not just being tired; it is the body shutting down and unable to do everyday things.

When this system is activated, you might feel disconnected or like you have collapsed. You can feel ill and depressed. You can feel numb, helpless, hopeless and trapped. You have low or zero energy and want to withdraw from people and events.

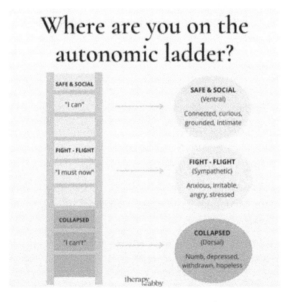

Diagram 1 – The Autonomic Ladder,
@therapywithabby on Instagram

When you get to know your nervous system and its different states, you can check in with yourself and see where you are on the ladder, as in Diagram 1.

The next step is to learn how to regulate yourself back up the ladder using self-soothing strategies.

How Do You Regulate Your Nervous System?

This is not easy when emotional attachment, comfort and soothing were not offered to you by your caregivers.

Below are some suggestions for self-soothing strategies that you could try to help bring your body back to a feeling of safety after being triggered.

- Cuddling a pet
- Spending time with one of your people
- Tossing a ball back and forth
- Going for a walk or run
- Laying your head on someone's lap
- Getting into nature and connecting with the ground, the sky, the river, and the trees – ground your feet, look up, and take in your surroundings through all your senses
- Singing, humming or chanting
- Dancing
- Listening to music
- Taking a warm bath
- Stretching – move those stuck energies around your body
- Watching a funny video

- Offering yourself some compassionate touch, e.g. hold your hands over your heart
- Rubbing your temples or any area that is holding tension
- Doing Yoga Nidra or Qigong
- Wearing something snuggly or laying down with a soft blanket
- Looking around the room and noticing – what can you hear, see, smell and touch?
- Smelling an essential oil
- Showing yourself loving kindness.

Breathwork

Breathwork is essential in mind-body connection work, and I would recommend you try it so you can begin to connect with your breath.

"Most of us have experienced mental, emotional or physical trauma on some level, which can restrict our breathing and capacity to feel. You may distract, numb, check out or disassociate when experiencing trauma or when triggered by past trauma.

I always recommend going slowly and working at your own pace.

The breath is your anchor to bring awareness to your senses, which at times can feel overwhelming."

Rebecca Dennis, *Let It Go, Breathe Yourself Calm*.

You can find breathwork sessions with Rebecca on YouTube.

Proceed with caution and always consider how you feel. Are you ready for this? How do you feel during it? You can always come back to it at another time.

Try different self-soothing strategies and see which are effective for you. Which strategies comfort you? Which give you the peace you need? Which bring you back into the present moment?

Start to become aware when your brain is looking for something to take the pain away and try a self-soothing strategy instead. Your brain may fight you and try to lead you to non-healthy strategies like food, alcohol, shopping, gambling, over-working and over-exercising to ease your emotional pain.

My non-healthy strategies are emotional eating, online shopping and over-working. When I feel myself defaulting to these strategies I try to pause and think about my needs, but it is a work in progress. I take it day by day and try to be really compassionate with myself.

Instead of unhealthy strategies, connect with your body. See what comes up when you ask yourself "What do I need?"

"Using the body as a portal to change automatic responses helps to remove the filters of the past, and allows you to see present-moment reality. It brings a freedom to live in the here and now. This is what helps you to flourish and thrive"

Jessica Maguire
@repairing_the_nervous_system on Instagram

Nine Tips for Starting to Connect Your Mind and Your Body

1. Start to become aware of how you treat your body.
2. Start to develop a relationship with your body. Get to know the messages your body is sending you.
3. Start to be conscious of how you feel different emotions in your body.
4. Be kind to your body. Develop an appreciation for what your body has done for you.
5. Get to know your nervous system and the different states.
6. Check in regularly and see where you are on the nervous system ladder.
7. Try some self-soothing strategies to help soothe your nervous system.
8. Try some breathwork.
9. Always go at your own pace and treat yourself with the utmost compassion.

CHAPTER EIGHT

Learning How to Feel

"When you are constantly feeling triggered, your day-to-day life and relationships are affected, and you feel out of control. It's like being in the ocean in a storm, in a small lifeboat with no oars and no life preserver, fearing for your life."

Lynne Friedman-Gell, PHD and Joanne Barron PSYD,
Intergenerational Trauma Workbook, Strategies to Support
Your Journey of Discovery, Growth and Healing

This quote describes what it felt like in my head during my 40s when memories of my past were coming up and banging me on the head. They yelled, "Deal with me," but I tried to ignore them. I couldn't understand why these memories were coming up. Most were from my childhood, but some right up to my 40s too. I had a sense that things were never going to change, let alone stop.

Every morning I woke up around 3 am, and it was like repeatedly listening to the same stories on a loop. It was exhausting and painful.

"Most of these events were so long ago."

"I should just get over them."

"I should move on."

So many invalidating thoughts were going around my head. I had been able to put a lid on these past events until now, but they would not go away, however hard I tried.

I had no idea what was happening. The confusion further exacerbated my ill health. I didn't know what to do with all these memories. It was like they had happened yesterday. They felt so current.

My head was full of thoughts and pain. My head hurt all the time. **ALL** the time.

I did not know then that wounds and trauma emerge for healing during the perimenopausal and menopausal years. Knowing this would have helped me at least understand why this was happening.

I now realise that I had stopped feeling. If I didn't feel, nothing could hurt me. But, not feeling meant I didn't feel happiness or joy either.

I was numb. Completely numb.

Why Do People Ignore Their Feelings?

They want to feel in control of themselves and their actions.

They don't want to feel upset.

They don't want to hurt.

They don't want to affect the people around them, so they pretend they're okay. How often are we sent the message, "Good vibes only"?

They don't want to face "negative" emotions. We are often sent the message that we should ignore the negative and focus on the positive.

They don't want to feel fragile or vulnerable.

They don't want to remember the past, so they avoid emotions and situations that might trigger them.

They then avoid emotions by avoiding conversations, people and things that might trigger them. They do anything to keep the emotion at a distance, out of harm's way.

If your caregivers couldn't or didn't love, care for you or meet your emotional needs, you stop seeking or expecting it, giving you no choice but to rely on yourself and become self-sufficient.

Your caregivers may have conveyed that emotions were unwelcome and would not be supported. This can result in considering facing your emotions as scary, dangerous and something to absolutely avoid.

Maybe you learned to suppress emotions to get love or to feel accepted.

Maybe you were belittled or even punished for showing emotions.

Even now, people in your life might try to talk you out of your feelings. They don't want you to feel bad; they are uncomfortable with how you are feeling; how you feel does not resonate with their feelings. It might be that they are not comfortable with you talking about past events.

You might even try to talk yourself out of your emotions with "positive thinking".

Are You Protecting Yourself by Pretending You Don't Have Feelings?

Bottling up, ignoring and repressing emotions leads to self-sufficiency and avoidance of feelings. It leads to not speaking up or advocating your needs and wants. It wreaks havoc on your nervous system. It increases anxiety and the chance of illness.

"Bottling is usually done with the best intentions, and to the practical person it does feel productive. 'Think positive', 'forge forward' and 'get on with it', we tell ourselves. And, poof, just like that, the unwanted emotions seem to vanish. But really they've just gone underground, ready to pop back up at any time, and usually with surprising and inappropriate intensity created by the containment pressure they've been under."

Susan David, *Emotional Agility, Get Unstuck, Embrace Change and Thrive in Work and Life*

Susan likens bottling and avoiding emotions to taking a painkiller to reduce physical pain. It has a short-term effect, but the pain soon returns.

Underneath all this suppressed emotion is a person. A person in pain. A person who yearns to be loved, wanted, and needed. A consistent and secure love that maybe you have never had before. You deserve this. You matter.

You also deserve to feel again. To feel the whole range of emotions rather than just those commonly spoken about.

The Range of Emotions

Brene Brown, in her book Atlas of the Heart, discusses the vast range of human emotions and emotional experiences. When you feel you have the headspace to take this in, you can take a look at the eighty-seven emotions listed on her website:

https://brenebrown.com/resources/atlas-of-the-heart-list-of-emotions

"Language is our portal to meaning-making, connection, healing, learning, and self-awareness. Having access to the right words can open up entire universes. When we don't have the language to talk about what we're experiencing, our ability to make sense of what's happening and share it with others is severely limited.

Without accurate language, we struggle to get the help we need, we don't always regulate or manage our emotions and experiences in a way that allows us to move through them productively, and our self-awareness is diminished. Language shows us that naming an experience doesn't give the experience more power, it gives us the power of understanding and meaning."

Brene Brown, *Atlas of the Heart, Mapping Meaningful Connection and the Language of Human Experience*

Knowing the full range of emotions allows us to understand and express how we are truly feeling.

Starting to Feel

"Naming an emotion might seem like a small thing- but for a lot of people it can be a BIG victory.

Lots of us have spent lots of time avoiding emotions. Being able to sit with our feelings, put words to them, not demand they change or go away – that's a BIG deal for a LOT of people"

Dr Glenn Doyle

The ultimate goal of being human is to feel, to feel ALL emotions, but it is essential to experience your feelings through a lens of safety. Get professional support if this work feels overwhelming or brings up too much for you to cope with.

Having feelings is entirely natural but proceed gently and with the utmost kindness and compassion for yourself.

You may not have allowed yourself to feel for a while.

You may not have thought much about how emotions feel in your body.

- Take a moment and consider how it feels in your body when you feel angry.
- How does your body feel when you are happy?
- What happens within your body when you feel irritated? When you feel sad?

Always take it easy. Go gently and at your own pace.

When feelings come up, notice them rather than push them away.

Sit in a quiet place with some soothing things around you and try this process:

1. Tune into your emotions without judging or trying to change them.
2. Listen to what the emotions are telling you – our feelings carry essential information that can help us change our lives for the better. Don't force this. Relax and see what comes up.
3. What are you feeling in your body? Welcome the feeling. You don't need to fight anymore.
4. Try responding to these emotions by checking in with yourself. What is the underlying need this emotion is bringing to your attention?

I like this exercise from Lynne Friedman-Gell and Joanne Barron's Intergenerational Trauma Workbook:

"When I feel (emotion), I (physical response).

And then I (current strategy to regulate my emotions).

A healthy strategy I could use instead is (a healthy adaptive strategy to regulate emotion)."

This allows you to check in with the emotion, how it feels in your body, how you currently react and how you would like to react in the future.

Treat yourself gently if you become aware when doing this work that you have been using unhealthy strategies to distract you from painful emotions. Common self-sabotaging strategies include turning to alcohol, emotional eating, overwork or isolating yourself. These are numbing strategies that can make you feel worse about yourself in the long run.

Think of your emotions like a good friend coming around for a coffee.

Create a loving environment that makes you feel warm and comfortable. Sit somewhere quiet and have some snuggly, comforting things around you. Then welcome your emotions, listen to them and have a kind, gentle, loving dialogue. Befriend your emotions.

Try to open your mind and allow what comes up. Don't resist or fight it.

"Hi, how are you today? Oh, hi, anger. I can feel you in my clenched jaw and my tense shoulders. Why are you here? Oh, you are telling me I am feeling disappointed and angry. Thank you for letting me know. It helps me see what has been going on for me. I can see I need to go out for a relaxing walk in nature to give me the chance to think about this more. This will stop me from buying something online to distract myself from disappointment. I can also see that it is valid and okay for me to feel this way, given what has happened in my past. Thank you."

Your body will need to build up a tolerance to this work. Don't push it. Listen to your body and take any action. If you feel overwhelmed or unsafe at any time, stop and do a self-soothing strategy, like breathwork.

Emotions showing up can mean that your body feels safe enough to feel them. When we can feel our emotions, we can start to process and move through them.

We are not in control of when emotions show up. They may show up when we cannot do this inner work or when it is not appropriate to react, for example, at work. But you can reflect later when you have some space for yourself.

Suppressed Emotions

Suppressed emotions come through as pain.

The pain is saying, "NOTICE ME! DO SOMETHING!"

If you ignore the pain, it will shout louder, giving you more pain.

Letting emotions in and sitting with them means potentially opening yourself up to hurt, to memories that you have hidden away for fear of going there. Proceed with great caution and get professional help from a trauma specialist or a psychotherapist to guide you.

"Suppressed emotions can come out in different ways. They can produce physical or mental illness; they can become under-expressed (hypoarousal, or numbness and dissociation) or over-expressed (hyperarousal, that is, agitation, panic, anger, rage or anxiety)."

Lynne Friedman-Gell, PHD and Joanne Barron PSYD,
Intergenerational Trauma Workbook, Strategies to Support Your Journey of Discovery, Growth and Healing

I had spent a lifetime batting away my emotions, telling myself it wasn't that bad, that I was wrong for feeling the way I was feeling.

I questioned myself. I doubted myself and my memories. This was exacerbated by trying to raise things with the people involved and getting knocked back.

There was never an acknowledgement or admission, and certainly no apology.

I was in a constant internal fight. Was I wrong? Was I being oversensitive? Why did my version of reality differ from theirs?

I knew how I felt and what I experienced, but without validation from others, I was left in a constant state of feeling confused. I felt like I was going mad. I didn't know how to deal with it. I had memories popping up left, right, and centre, memories that were causing me real pain up to 40 years after the event.

I stuffed the painful memories and emotions down. No, I didn't want to go there. I would and could pretend that things were okay until it all came tumbling down again. I lived my life in a cycle of pain.

I wasn't listening to my body. I was fighting my body. I was beating it up. I was ignoring every signal it was sending me.

After my breakdown, I worked with a homeopath, who is also a mind-body therapist, and she introduced me to the concept of feeling emotions in my body. It took some time. I hadn't "felt" for a long time. I had numbed myself. I had blocked my feelings.

I worked on the process with her initially and then used it myself between sessions.

Feeling was scary and overwhelming. If I felt I might have to admit what happened to me, I might have to do something about it. It felt easier to store it away, but back then, I had no idea that storing it away was causing my physical pain.

Anger

The emotion I struggled with more than any other was anger.

I am not an angry person.

When I was younger, I took pride in being level-headed and calm. I was the steady one, the "good" child. I now know that this was to protect myself in an emotionally volatile environment.

I became quiet and unemotional to protect myself. I hated conflict. I stuffed my personality and feelings away to keep the peace.

If I pleased everyone life would be okay. I would not have to walk on eggshells. I would not have to sit in silence. It was like someone pressed the pause button on the TV, and you could not live or enjoy anything until normal service was resumed.

"Anger is a beautiful, necessary catalyst for change. But anger needs to ignite something. It's a terrible lifetime companion. But it is a very important catalyst to change. When we see something that is unfair, unjust, lacks equity, our response of anger is what fuels change. But to stay in it perpetually, there's a lot of physical, emotional and spiritual costs."

Brene Brown

Behind your anger could be feelings of fear, loneliness, rejection, frustration, confusion, hurt, grief, sadness, guilt, shame, jealousy etc.

So, how does a calm, steady person express anger without affecting others?

I hit a pillow.

I shout into a cushion.

I move around and shake to move the energies around my body. I let the tension, anger, and hurt out of my body. I don't want them inside of me anymore.

I shout (but not at anyone) – I go into the middle of a field (checking that no one is there first!) and let it out.

I stand by the river and imagine the anger inside me as a colour, letting it out. I don't plan how it will happen; instead, I see what comes up when I quiet down and listen. Sometimes it's black and comes out of my nose, sometimes it's purple and comes out of my ears!

My anger was telling me that things weren't right. That I didn't deserve to be treated the way I was. I learned that it was okay to be angry and that I had every right to feel angry.

I learned that it was okay to let it out. It was crucial to let it out. Those suppressed emotions had caused me so much mental and physical pain: feelings that had been within me, bottled up, some from the age of seven.

I also learned how to experience and process guilt, disappointment, grief and shame, to name a few other emotions. Processing these emotions has allowed me to shift a lot of the trauma.

I have learned that emotions come and go, that they are essential and that allowing them in is vital for my well-being and future happiness.

I see myself as the endless sky and my emotions as the clouds. Sometimes the clouds are thick, dark, and heavy, sometimes the clouds are light, but they are all temporary.

Letting your emotions in means dealing with some painful memories when you are ready. Doing this work with emotional safety and support will relieve pain and allow you to feel again – to feel the whole gamut of emotions and live. I now know what it feels like to feel happiness and joy. I can feel my heart open when I experience joy.

But I will never diminish how hard it is to feel your feelings, to let emotions in.

It is challenging after years of suppressing yourself, but it is part of feeling human again, and I hope you can begin to feel again – to feel the whole range of human emotions. It is crucial for you, your well-being and your healing.

> "If she got really quiet and listened, new parts of her wanted to speak."

Sark,
https://www.facebook.com/PlanetSARK

Seven Tips for Learning How to Feel

1. Make a regular habit of checking in with your emotions. You can do this at a set time of day or when an emotion comes up.
2. Take some time in a quiet place and sit with the emotion. How are you feeling? How does the emotion feel in your body?
3. Ask yourself if there is any action you need to take.
4. You could journal what is coming up for you.
5. After letting your emotions in, offer yourself compassion and love. You may feel drained afterwards.
6. You could offer yourself some compassionate touch, e.g. holding your hand to your heart to soothe yourself.
7. Seek professional help from a trauma-informed practitioner to support you with challenging memories coming up or if you are feeling overwhelmed.

CHAPTER NINE

Moving from People-Pleasing to Setting Boundaries

Do you put other people's needs before your own?

Do you put pressure on yourself to please others?

Do you overexplain?

Are you overly polite?

Do you avoid conflict?

These are big questions.

Be kind and gentle with yourself as you contemplate them.

I did all of the above and more, but I didn't realise it at the time. Looking back, it alarms me to realise what I was doing. I glorified being busy and now realise that I kept myself busy, so I didn't have time to think.

As my health worsened during my 40s, I was running myself ragged trying to be all things to all people but forgot myself in the process. All I wanted to do was please others. I was looking to other people to give me love, acknowledgement, a sense of belonging and validation.

I don't think I knew who I was anymore. I don't think there was a 'me' anymore.

I often felt annoyed that some people didn't do things for me that I so readily did for them. That others didn't treat me the way I treated them. I found myself starting to resent people. Some people in my life were taking advantage of my good nature – and my complete lack of boundaries! - and not doing anything for me in return.

I was not only exhausted but hurt. I didn't know how to deal with it. I didn't know how to put a stop to it. I didn't know how to speak up for myself. I felt stuck. Stuck in a prison of perpetual people-pleasing.

I was searching for acknowledgement and a sense of belonging. On reflection, I can see that I was working myself to the bone – both at work and in my relationships – to get tiny glimmers of love and praise. Each time they didn't come, I went under until the weight of it all became too much, and I had my breakdown.

You, too, may have grown up feeling you had no choice and couldn't say no to anyone.

It is not easy to suddenly make choices or say to no to anyone when your needs were never seen as important. I completely hear you on this. It became a revelation when my psychotherapist started talking to me about choice and setting boundaries. I had no idea that I had a choice. I had to proceed gently. It took time and practice to feel confident and competent in making choices and setting boundaries.

Being able to assert your choices and to say no come from a place of self-worth. But self-worth is often very low for those who were raised in an emotionally dysfunctional family.

Developing self-worth takes time. It also takes practice, support and patience.

"When you're not used to being confident, confidence feels like arrogance.

When you're used to being passive, assertiveness feels like aggression.

When you're not used to getting your needs met, prioritizing yourself feels selfish."

@junocounselling on Instagram

What is People-Pleasing?

People-pleasing is an underlying urge to make others happy, to be liked and well thought of.

It is natural to want others to be happy, but people-pleasers dive deeply into other people's needs at the expense of their own needs and desires.

In the act of people-pleasing, you negate yourself and your needs and focus on the other person. You are working hard to get your worth from the other person rather than seeing your worth.

Don't criticize yourself for people-pleasing in the past.

People-pleasing is a nervous system response.

Children brought up in emotionally dysfunctional families often people-please to feel some attachment with their caregivers and to avoid further emotional unrest or conflict.

The first step in moving away from people-pleasing is becoming
aware of your tendency to put others before yourself. The aim
is for you to be able to express yourself honestly and do what is
right for you. This will take time.

It feels familiar and safe to stay people-pleasing, but you can
overcome this by becoming aware of your needs and learning
about your boundaries.

What are the Consequences of People-Pleasing?

When you are people-pleasing and focusing on the happiness or
approval of others, you are:

- Disconnecting from yourself
- Going against your gut instinct
- Repressing yourself
- Making the other person more important than you
- Sending the message that their happiness is more
  important than yours.

Trying to please everyone leaves you with little time or energy
to take care of yourself.

You may find yourself morphing into the version of you that you
think the other person wants. There could be different versions
of you depending on who you are with.

You may end up in one-sided relationships where you end up
being the person people turn to but where you don't get the
same in return. You may find that some of your relationships can
be short-lived.

People-pleasing can mean you are constantly on the go, rushing around doing things for other people, leaving you little, if any, time for yourself. This can lead to exhaustion and burnout.

Time Wealth

I learned about the concept of time wealth from Dr Emma Hepburn @ThePsychologyMum on Instagram. This concept resonated with me and encouraged me to start valuing my time rather than giving it away freely.

I now see my time as a precious commodity. I make sure there are free days in my diary and free time in my day. Time to do things for me.

Think about your time:

- If you have a free moment in the day, do you rush to fill it?
- If someone asks if you are free, do you do everything to give them some of your time?
- Do you feel you have to say yes to others when you don't have something else already scheduled?

Start to become mindful of your time without any judgement.

Your time is precious.

You are precious.

Start to appreciate that you don't get your time back once you give it away.

By protecting your time, you are thinking about your needs, and you are also protecting your stress levels and reducing feelings of overwhelm.

Protecting your time and scheduling time for you is self-compassion and self-care. It is not being selfish.

When you give your time away, you miss out on time for yourself. You miss out on the chance to rest.

The Importance of Rest

The definition of rest is to cease work or movement to relax (sleep) or recover strength. This is important, but many people think that they are not doing anything when they are resting.

You ARE doing something, you are RESTING, and rest is vital for your mental, emotional and physical well-being.

You are NOT being lazy if you rest.

Value your rest time. Don't gift that time to others.

"I lied and said I was busy.

I was busy; but not in a way most people understand.

I was busy taking deeper breaths.

I was busy silencing irrational thoughts.

I was busy calming a racing heart.

I was busy telling myself I am okay.

Sometimes, this is my busy -

and I will not apologize for it."

Brittin Oakman,
seen on The Artidote Facebook page

We all need seven types of rest: physical, mental, emotional, social, sensory, creative and spiritual.

You can read more about the different types of rest online at:

https://blog.ed.ted.com/2021/02/08/the-7-types-of-rest-that-every-person-
needs/?msclkid=4740b4f6cfa811ec9e79aa3f7592b3f6

What are Boundaries?

Boundaries are a way of taking care of yourself.

"Boundaries are the protective and invisible parameters that separate you from the world; the distinctions between what's mine and what's yours. Boundaries relate to the ability to say no and consciously choose our involvement in activities, friendships, and what we'll tolerate based on our energy levels, time and capacity."

Amy B. Scher,
*How to Heal Yourself From Depression
When No One Else Can*

Boundaries protect you, your time and your health.

Boundaries show others how you expect and want to be treated.

Having boundaries is a sign of self-respect.

An example of a boundary is:

"Thank you for inviting me, but I need some time for myself."

Jake Ernst @mswjake states that there are five different boundary types and gives examples of each:

1. Mental – freedom to have your thoughts, beliefs, values and opinions, e.g. "We disagree on that."

2. Emotional – guidelines around how we want to be treated – e.g. "Please don't speak to me this way."

3. Physical – choice in how you engage with others through proximity, touch and intimacy, e.g. "I don't want to be touched that way."

4. Material – choice around possessions; how or when they can be used and how they are treated, e.g. "I'd prefer it if you wore your own clothes."

5. Quality of Life – how you spend your time, money and energy; includes downtime, routines, favours for other people, scheduling, your finances, e.g. "No, I don't have time to do that."

Why Do People Struggle with Boundaries?

The need for boundaries may cause distress and anxiety to those who were raised in a home:

- with a lack of boundaries.
- where they were taught that their needs didn't matter or came second to their caregiver.
- where they were made to feel responsible for others' happiness.

- where they weren't allowed to be their authentic self.

Boundaries are a challenge for compassionate people/empaths.

You may think it is rude to say no to someone.

You may feel guilty or anxious when setting a boundary.

You may be worried about hurting someone's feelings.

You may be worried about disappointing someone.

You may have no idea how to set a boundary.

It may be so out of your comfort zone that it feels easier not to set boundaries, but they are essential for your well-being.

"It might feel uncomfortable in the moment to set a boundary, but it's important to remember that a moment of discomfort can prevent long-lasting feelings of resentment, disappointment and anger."

@therapywithabby on Instagram

The Word "NO"

One way of asserting your boundaries is by saying no to something you don't want to do.

You may have seen the phrase, "No is a sentence", but saying "no" can cause anxiety for a people-pleaser.

Kerry Dunn @people.pleasers.rehab on Instagram shows how to build up your confidence when you want to say no:

Level 1	Not saying no
Level 2	A maybe
Level 3	Hinting at no
Level 4	A gentle no
Level 5	A hard no

How to Say "No" Without Saying the Word "No!"

"Thanks for asking, but it's not for me."

"I don't have the time."

"Thanks for thinking of me, but I have a lot on."

"I understand you would like me to be there, but I can't attend."

Also be aware that you don't have to reply to a text, email, or invitation immediately.

You don't have to make a quick decision.

Give yourself time and reply when it is right for you. Reply in the right way for you. No one should pressurise you for a quick response. If they do, you have every right to say you will get back to them.

There is no need to apologise when saying no, though you may feel more comfortable saying "sorry" or "I'm afraid" when first setting boundaries. With confidence, I hope you will be able to say no without feeling the need to apologise.

You don't have to justify your response.

Dunn talks about the difference between context and justifying when you want to say no.

She states that context shows why it's a no.

Context tells why but does not ask for approval.

"I can't make it. My diary is pretty full at the moment."

Justifying your no is asking for approval.

"I can't make it. I hope this is okay."

Contrary to what you may think, you don't need the other person's approval to say no.

Justifying can include overexplaining.

Do You Overexplain?

Overexplaining is when you go into lots of detail – TOO much detail.

Overexplaining can be a trauma response. It can result from a childhood in which you had to justify your choices.

People-pleasers tend to overexplain when they feel bad about saying no; subconsciously, it eases their guilt.

I used to get lost in a minefield of overexplaining. I couldn't say no or assert myself. I felt I had to do things. I would be anxious for days if asked to do something I didn't want to do. I would lose sleep over how to respond. I would overthink and then overexplain because I couldn't say how I felt. I would practise replies for a few days until I was happy with the response. I would ask others to help me as I didn't know what to do.

Next time you find yourself overexplaining, ask yourself if you are explaining or if you are going into lots of detail to ease your feelings of discomfort.

If the people in your life are used to you being a people-pleaser, they may struggle with you suddenly having boundaries. This does not mean that boundaries are a bad thing. It shows that they are needed. Stick with it. Journalling any feelings that come up can help you deal with any difficulties you experience when trying to set boundaries.

When Someone Asks You to Do Something

Ask yourself these questions:

- Do I WANT to do it? (If you don't want to do it, reflect on why you feel you should say yes.)
- Have I got the time to do it?
- Is it good for my mental health?

Give the answer that is right for you, not the other person.

As you strive to push through any complicated feelings, here are some affirmations that you can say to yourself that can be helpful reminders:

- I value and care for myself enough to do what is right for me.
- I have a right to do what is best for me.
- I have a choice.

- I have a right to change my mind.
- I have a right to say yes or no.
- I have a right to express my feelings.
- I have the right to decline responsibility for other people's issues and problems.
- I can have empathy but still have the right to do what is appropriate for me, without apology or explanation.

Why Boundaries are Important

Putting yourself first doesn't mean that you only care about yourself, and it doesn't mean that other people in your life aren't important. What it does mean is that you value and respect yourself.

"Far from being walls that keep everybody out, my boundaries are the lines that help me let the right ones in."

Molly Davis, Wild Goose Counselling,
https://www.facebook.com/WildGooseCounseling

Your safe people will support you whilst you do this work, but some people who are used to you being a people-pleaser may struggle when you start to have boundaries. They are used to you saying yes and putting their needs first. They may resist your attempts to set boundaries. They may try to persuade you otherwise. This is not a reason to stop. Keep going and keep practising. You can do this.

I will never diminish or underestimate how tough it can be to set boundaries and say no when you are a people-pleaser, but you can do this with time, practice and self-compassion.

I now know that boundaries are not only important, they are
crucial for my well-being.

It has taken time, practise and work, but now I do things because
I want to do them, not because I think I need or should do them
to make others happy. This is not being selfish. It is doing what
is right for me and my mental and emotional health, and I am
much happier and stronger for it.

Because I have clear boundaries, I no longer have those feelings
of resentment. People can't take advantage of my kind nature
because I have boundaries to protect myself.

Occasionally I can sense the old people-pleaser in me trying to
come back, but then I pause and reflect. I honour myself, my
needs and my time.

There are some excellent books and social media accounts that
offer advice on people-pleasing and boundary setting. Please
see the References and Additional Resources at the end of the
book when you feel ready to find out more.

"The root of self-care is setting boundaries."

Nedra Glover Tawwab,
Set Boundaries, Find Peace,
A Guide to Reclaiming Yourself

Seven Tips for Starting to Move from People-Pleasing to Setting Boundaries

1. Become aware of when you people-please and treat yourself with compassion.

2. Start to value your time – don't give it away easily.

3. Schedule rest time for yourself.

4. Practise setting boundaries with your safe people.

5. Practise saying no in safe environments.

6. Be mindful of when you overexplain and try to be more concise. Reflect on whether the information that you are sharing is necessary.

7. When someone asks you to do something you don't want to do, ask yourself if you really want to do it and then reply accordingly.

CHAPTER TEN

Opening your Heart to Self-Compassion

Have you ever thought about how you treat yourself?

Have you ever paid attention to how you speak to yourself. That internal voice – commonly known as the inner critic – that speaks up when you make a mistake, if you drop something, if you don't like how you look in the mirror, or if something doesn't go as planned?

Be kind and compassionate with yourself as you think about this.

You may never have paid attention to how you treat yourself.

You may not have considered that you can change your internal critical voice into a voice of kindness, compassion and support, a nurturing voice that encourages and motivates you. A voice that is gentle and understanding, especially when life is tough.

You might think it impossible, but you can change your relationship with yourself. You can learn to treat yourself with the same kindness you so readily give to others.

The person that you spend the most time with is.....YOU.

Your relationship with yourself is THE most important one you will ever have.

What do they tell you when you fly? That you must put YOUR lifejacket on first in an emergency.

Needs and Values

"The fundamental self-compassion question is 'What do I need?' But we can't really give ourselves what we need if we don't know what we value most in our lives. These are our core values, those deeply held ideals that guide us and give meaning to our lives.

Both needs and values seem to reflect something essential in human nature. Needs are more commonly associated with physical and emotional survival, such as the need for health and safety, or for love and connection, whereas values tend to have an element of choice, such as the choice to focus on social justice of creative pursuits."

Kristin Neff, PhD and Christopher Germer, PhD,
The Mindful Self-Compassion Workbook, A Proven Way to Accept Yourself, Build Inner Strength, and Thrive

What are Values?

Values are the things that you believe are important, the things that are valuable to you.

- Values are intrinsic to you.
- Your values are as distinctly yours as your thumbprint.
- They are part of your identity.
- They are what make you, you.

When the things you do and the way you behave match your values, life is usually good, but things can feel very wrong when they don't align with your values.

As you move through life, your values may change as you change and evolve as a person.

When you know your values, you discover what's truly important to you, what makes you tick, and what makes your soul sing.

"Values are a life lived fully from the inside out."

Henry Kimsey-House, Karen Kimsey-House, Phillip Sandahl,
Laura Whitworth,
Co-Active Coaching, The Proven Framework for
Transformative Conversations at Work and in Life

Discovering Your Values

Look at the list of values below and highlight those important to you, those that reflect you and what matters to you. The values that are important to YOU.

Then go back through the list and circle those that are of greatest priority to you right now.

Knowing your values helps you make the right decisions and reflect on how you want your life to be.

Once you know your values, you can be more proactive in how you live your life. When you make decisions, you can ask yourself if they align with your values.

Accomplishment	Discipline	Independence	Privacy
Achievement	Discovery	Inner peace	Relationships
Adventure	Diversity	Job security	Respect
Authenticity	Empowerment	Joy	Safety
Balance	Environment	Kindness	Security
Beauty	Equality	Knowledge	Self-discipline
Being the best	Fairness	Leadership	Self-expression
Belonging	Faith	Learning	Spontaneity
Calm	Family	Leisure	Status
Career	Financial Stability	Love	Success
Change	Freedom	Meaning	Thrift
Comfort	Friendship	Nature	Time
Community	Fun	Openness	Travel
Compassion	Generosity	Order	Trust
Confidence	Giving back	Parenting	Uniqueness
Connection	Growth	Passion	Unity
Contentment	Happiness	Peace	Variety
Courage	Hard work	Personal choice	Wellbeing
Creativity	Improvement	Pleasure	Wholeheartedness

Adapted from a longer list of values by Lori Fitzgerald at the Therapy Den. https://www.facebook.com/therapydenonline

Becoming more aware of your values can help you make better choices in different situations.

Knowing and living by your values can help you to reconnect with yourself.

Why Do I Find it Hard to be Caring and Compassionate with Myself?

To be compassionate with yourself, you must feel that you matter and deserve to be treated well.

This can be tough for people who didn't have unconditional love as a child, were accustomed to putting the needs of others before their own, and stifled their personalities to keep the peace. That loss of self takes its toll.

"The idea of self-care can be foreign to some or seem impossible. The quality of care and nurturing you received as a child forms the template for how you take care of yourself as you grow up. So, if your needs were not adequately met when you were young, it may be difficult for you to prioritize self-care as an adult. In addition, unresolved trauma may keep you from being unaware of what you need, want, or feel."

Lynne Friedman-Gell, PHD and Joanne Barron, PSYD,
Intergenerational Trauma Workbook, Strategies to Support Your Journey of Discovery, Growth, and Healing

You may have been brought up by a caregiver who:

- did not give you caring and nurturing touch. Touch that would offer reassurance and help you feel safe, warm and connected.
- could not soothe their nervous system, so you didn't learn how to soothe your own system.
- could not sit with and cope with your emotions, as they couldn't cope with their own.
- didn't see their value and told you that it was selfish to look after yourself.

It can feel challenging, if not impossible, to prioritise yourself if you weren't made to feel important, or if you weren't loved and supported unconditionally.

You may have grown up thinking that there are expectations around you, that you are responsible for others, or that it's your job to run around looking after everyone else.

"It (childhood trauma) can make it harder to have self-compassion as adults as feelings of love and care become fused with feelings of fear and pain early on. With the help of mental health professionals, we can learn to be compassionate toward our early trauma, giving us more ability to cope with the enormity of our pain. In many ways what's occurring is that we are re-parenting ourselves, giving ourselves the unconditional love, care and safety that we didn't receive as kids. Although it takes time, through consistent practice of self-compassion we can eventually develop secure attachment as adults. We can learn to rely on our own warmth and support as a source of safety, providing the stable platform needed to take on life's challenges."

Kristin Neff, Fierce Self-Compassion,
How Women Can Harness Kindness to Speak Up,
Claim Their Power and Thrive

You can begin to show yourself compassion by:

Showing care for the younger you who suffered.

Chatting to the younger you and letting her know you are there for her.

Acknowledging what happened to the younger you and empathising with how she felt.

Giving the younger you the unconditional love and support she needed.

Giving "adult" you the love and support you need.

Being your number one cheerleader.

Once you start living by your values and being kinder to yourself, you will see your worth. It takes time and practice, but you deserve to feel special.

You ARE special.

You deserve that love, care and compassion you offer others.

What is Compassion?

Compassion means "to suffer together". The definition of compassion is the "pity and concern for the suffering or misfortunes of others".

Compassion, for me, is kind-heartedness, warmth, care, empathy and understanding.

It is an emotion or feeling but also a need to reduce someone's suffering.

I consider compassion vital to living a whole and enriched life. I now approach all aspects of my life with compassion, but this was not the case before my breakdown. I didn't even make the list of people that were important in my life. Now I am at the top of that list!

What is Self-Compassion?

Self-compassion is treating yourself as kindly as you would a friend or a loved one.

It is about comforting and caring for yourself during difficult times rather than turning against yourself.

It is about living by and honouring your values.

It is about honouring and protecting yourself and your needs.

Kristin Neff is Associate Professor of Educational Psychology at the University of Texas at Austin. She runs the Center for Mindful Self-Compassion and is a pioneer in self-compassion research, conducting the first empirical studies on self-compassion almost twenty years ago.

She states that there are three elements to self-compassion:

1. Self-Kindness – "being warm and understanding towards ourselves when we suffer, fail or feel inadequate"
2. Common Humanity – "recognising that suffering and personal inadequacy is part of the shared human experience"
3. Mindfulness – "a non-judgmental, receptive mind state in which one observes thoughts and feelings as they are, without trying to suppress or deny them."

Self-compassion is accepting yourself as you are right now with compassion and kindness.

You can test your current level of self-compassion on Kristin Neff's website at:
https://self-compassion.org/self-compassion-test/.

Be kind and gentle with yourself with what comes up during the test. You can work on this with the utmost compassion for yourself. You can become your own best friend. It will take time and practice, but it is possible.

There are also self-compassion exercises that you can try on Kristin's website.

"Self-Compassion is Life-Changing."

I know this to be true as self-compassion has changed my life.

Every aspect of my life has benefited from it. Everyone in my life has benefited from it.

Kristin Neff said these exact words during a course I took with her in 2022.

I shall repeat them:

"Self-compassion is life-changing."

I now have a warm inner voice and am much kinder to myself. If I hear myself saying something unkind to myself, for example, saying I am an idiot if I drop something, I now have a chat with my inner voice and say that I am not an idiot. I dropped it because I was rushing around, trying to do too many things at once and that I am human.

Sometimes I look at myself in the mirror and default to negative comments on my perceived faults and flaws. But when this happens, I now interrupt myself and speak appreciatively about myself.

I have developed an appreciation and acceptance of myself. I embrace my uniqueness. I still hear negative self-talk and know I am a work in progress, but I now have empathetic chats with myself. I no longer berate myself. I am gentle and understanding, just as I would be with a friend.

Compassionate Self-Talk

Compassionate self-talk takes regular practice after years of negativity.

Sometimes you may not fully believe the positive things you are saying to yourself. You may resist it, but keep going until you know it, believe it, and own it.

Try repeating affirmations like these daily:

- I am worthy.
- I am lovable.
- I deserve to be loved for who I am.
- I am enough.
- I have always been enough.

The more you say these things to yourself, the more you will begin to internalise them and believe them. Be consistent with this practice. Make it a regular ritual.

If these affirmations feel too much for you at this time, try some neutral affirmations like:

- I am trying.
- I am doing okay.
- I'll do what I can today.

If you struggle to think of positive things about yourself, ask "your people" to tell you what they love about you. Keep a copy or note down their responses and read them regularly.

When I was a teacher at the beginning of my working life, I had a difficult experience with a parent. The Head Teacher was hugely supportive and gave me this advice: if someone gives you a card or letter with a lovely personal message (this was before the days of emails and texts!), keep them together in a safe place.

I would recommend that you do something similar, and then if you are feeling down or have been criticised, look at the messages and remember your worth and how valued you are.

To this day, I have a folder of "lovely messages" which I read on both good and down days. They never fail to warm my heart, make me smile, and remind me that I am loved and appreciated.

It can be an actual folder or an album of photos and screenshots on your phone.

These messages can be your light on a dark day. They can remind you of your value if you forget. They remind you to treat yourself with compassion.

Prioritise You and Your Wellbeing

Start to take an active role in looking after yourself and your wellbeing.

Make you your priority.

Introduce some self-compassion habits into your daily life and be consistent. Here are some exercises you can try:

- Become aware of the things that make you happy and do them more often.

- Become aware of the things that soothe you and do them more often.
- Start appreciating yourself more.
- Check in with your values regularly.
- Practise daily affirmations.
- Schedule in time just for you.
- Allow yourself to rest.
- Do what is right for you, not for others.

During my darkest times, I loathed myself and bullied myself regularly. I had completely lost myself and was constantly pointing out my perceived flaws, faults and lack of ability to myself.

Nothing about me was good enough. It was painful. The constant chatter in my head was exhausting.

I now give myself that validation. I provide myself with compassion and love. This does not mean that I don't want or need strokes of love and acknowledgement from others, but it means I can rely on myself to be kind, loving, and to give myself what I need.

When self-compassionate, you are validating your thoughts and experiences, not fighting them. You are no longer battling against yourself, berating yourself, or bullying yourself. There is no longer a constant fight in your head – a fight that causes pain and anguish. You are on your side.

It has been a long process to get here, and I still need to practise it daily, but my relationship with myself and my view of myself has improved ten-fold.

By treating ourselves well, we develop inner strength and confidence to become fiercer, speak up, assert our needs, etc.

What are the Benefits of Self-Compassion?

Self-compassion has so many long-lasting impacts on your life. Here are some of them.

Self-compassion will:

- reduce negative feelings about yourself
- boost your happiness
- give you increased hope
- encourage connection with others
- allow you to regulate your emotions
- lead to improved physical and mental health
- be a source of inner strength
- boost your confidence
- give you courage and greater resilience when facing challenges and difficulties.

Self-compassion makes all aspects of your life better. So, start gently and practise self-compassion regularly.

Proceed carefully, make it manageable and achievable and always act with love and compassion for yourself. Don't let this be something that further adds to your emotional load. It is vital work, and you are worthy of it.

"I learned a long time ago the wisest thing I can do is be on my own side."

Maya Angelou

Ten Tips for Opening Your Heart to Self-Compassion

1. Find out what is important to you by doing the values exercise.
2. Become mindful of how you treat yourself. Do this with kindness and compassion towards yourself.
3. Become mindful of how you talk about yourself.
4. Take the Self-Compassion Test at:
   https://selfcompassion.org./self-compassion-test/
5. Start to talk to yourself with more compassion.
6. Say the positive affirmations to yourself daily.
7. Build up a bank of positive messages about yourself.
8. Start to prioritise yourself and your wellbeing.
9. Treat yourself with compassion.
10. Journal about how you are getting on with bringing self-compassion into your life, including any changes you are noticing.

CHAPTER ELEVEN
Getting to Know Yourself

"Does it seem strange to think about spending time on developing a relationship with yourself? You might think, *I am always myself; why would I need to work on a relationship with myself? What would that even look like?* But it's the most foundational relationship you have; it determines your happiness, success, and genuine connection with other people."

Lindsay C. Gibson, PsyD,
Recovering from Emotionally Immature Parents,
Practical Tools to Establish Boundaries
and Reclaim Your Emotional Autonomy

Reflecting on the lead-up to my breakdown, I realised I had completely lost my sense of self. I wasn't doing anything for myself. I wasn't taking care of myself. I wasn't valuing myself. I was bullying myself regularly without being aware of it. I was physically and mentally very ill. I was in a lot of pain. I was exhausted, and life felt tough, so very tough.

I wasn't giving myself any attention and certainly didn't think about my relationship with myself.

If you had told me I could change things, that I could change my relationship with myself, I wouldn't have believed you.

Looking back and acknowledging how little I cared for myself was tough. It had been this way for a long time, for longer than I would like to admit.

How Do You See Yourself?

How you see yourself begins in your childhood.

When you are a child, you learn about yourself through the eyes of your caregivers and their lens on life.

If your family lacks emotional maturity and you feel like you don't belong, you spend your life looking to fit somewhere – anywhere – and you so desperately want to be loved. If that means changing to fit in, you do it because you want someone to give you that feeling of unconditional love and emotional connection you have always missed, wanted, and needed.

If you are brought up to put the needs of your caregivers before your own, you spend all your emotional energy being everything and anything but yourself. You forget about yourself and your needs and get your worth from others instead of yourself.

Maybe you were from a family where you weren't allowed to be an individual with wants and needs and were strongly encouraged or forced to follow the family norms, where you were told how to be and that your choices were wrong.

Living in an environment like this has a massive impact. You may adapt yourself to fit in with the family norms. You may morph yourself into what you think is expected of you. You may quash aspects of your personality to be accepted. You may be quiet to keep the peace.

You may think that something is inherently wrong with you, so you change into a version of yourself that you think is acceptable to others.

For some people, you may be too much; for others, not enough. I want to make it clear that you are not too much and that you have always been enough, contrary to any messages you may have been given.

You work hard to get your value and your worth from your job, from the money you earn, from the different roles you play in life, for example, Mum, wife, daughter; from your responsibilities, your friendships, your body, your mind, your personality, your past, your successes, your productivity, from other's opinions and your expectations.

As your confidence decreases, you start to make yourself and your world small to protect yourself from the outside world. You play it safe. You limit yourself. For example, you stay in a job that isn't making you happy because you don't think you can do anything else.

You accept treatment that reminds you of how you were treated when you were younger. This feels familiar to you. You stay in a relationship or friendship because you don't think you deserve better.

You exhaust yourself by being everything for everyone else whilst neglecting yourself. I was going to add that you neglect your needs too, but you may not know what your needs are or that you even have any needs. You focus on the needs of others and forget yourself. Who are you to have needs? You don't feel worthy of having needs.

"If you don't see yourself as worthy, you won't take charge when you need to. If you don't find yourself interesting, how will you promote yourself or have close, rewarding relationships with others? If you aren't self-protective, how can you feel safe with someone?"

Lindsay C. Gibson, PsyD,
Recovering from Emotionally Immature Parents,
Practical Tools to Establish Boundaries
and Reclaim Your Emotional Autonomy

It was only after my breakdown that I started to think about how I treated myself.

I was a people-pleaser who morphed into a version of me that I thought the other person found acceptable. I changed depending on who I was with. I didn't know myself anymore. I am unsure where the real me went, but I disconnected from her at a young age when I began to change to keep the peace.

I have reconnected with young Victoria during the last few years. She is gorgeous and such a little star. She had a mischievousness that she tucked away. She had a zest for life and an inner spark that she had to hide because these traits weren't acceptable to others. I have little chats with her and reassure her that we have each other's backs now. I let her know that there was never anything wrong with her.

Developing a Relationship with Yourself

I now know that the most important relationship I will ever have is with myself. But I must point out that it is not easy to focus on yourself when you have been sent the message that you are not important or good enough or that something is wrong with you. Be gentle with yourself and take it slowly and steadily. It takes time and work to develop your sense of self again, but it can be exciting and fun.

Now is the time to focus on you, to think about you separate from your family, your childhood and your past.

YOU.

Not what others want of you.

This is all about YOU and what YOU want.

With kindness and compassion, you can become aware of how you currently see yourself and consider why you think this way. Professional support can be invaluable in this process.

"'Finding yourself' is not really how it works. You aren't a ten-dollar bill in last winter's coat pocket. You are also not lost. Your true self is right there, buried under cultural conditioning, other people's opinions, and inaccurate conclusions you drew as a kid that became your beliefs about who you are. 'Finding yourself' is actually returning to yourself. An unlearning, an excavation, a remembering who you were before the world got its hands on you."

Emily McDowell

Start by reconnecting with times when you felt happiness or experienced joy. Take some time on your own and start to think about joyful times. You can journal what comes up.

Think back through different ages and stages of your life and connect with what made you happy at those times. It could be music you listened to, TV programmes you watched, a concert you went to, a place you visited, or people in your life who you loved being around.

I did an exercise like this when undertaking a free online course with a coach, and it helped me look at the positive times rather than my mind being full of the difficult times.

Think about people in your past who made you happy. This could be a relative, teacher, boss, friend etc. Were there people you felt comfortable being around? People you used to love spending time with. People who made you feel loved and enough.

This exercise can bring joy and positivity, and optimism. It may also bring up sadness at how others treated you. Be gentle and compassionate with yourself and always seek support if required.

You could play a piece of music that you loved. See what memories and emotions it evokes and how you feel. Dance to the music. Does it bring back joy and happiness, even for a few minutes? Reconnect with those happy feelings and how they feel within your body.

Look at photos from happy times. What was it that made you happy? Was it the people you were around, the place, or the environment or situation?

Another way of reconnecting with the core of you is to know your values. See Chapter 10 for a values exercise.

This work may feel egotistical at first – work like this can feel selfish for someone who didn't feel worthy of love as a child.

Once you start to see your value and appreciate yourself with compassion for what happened and its effect on you, it will feel more natural.

I started slowly and gently by making a scrapbook of myself.

I had pages in my scrapbook entitled:

- Things I love to do
- Things I do for self-care
- I am.... (positive qualities)
- I like to eat....
- People I love being around....
- Places I love.......

I wrote lists for each and printed off photos and quotes. It became a joyful, creative, and calming activity. A journal would also work well, as would using Pinterest or creating a photo album on your mobile device.

Doing this helped me focus on the happy and joyful people and memories. When you are struggling, your mind is awash with difficult memories. Putting a focus on positive memories is nurturing and motivating and gives you glimmers of hope.

Hope that you can be happy again.

Hope that things can change.

Hope that there are good times ahead for you.

Creating my scrapbook was a joyous exercise in developing my sense of self again. I started to listen to music more. I realised I stopped doing things that used to bring me so much happiness when I was ill. Reconnecting with music and creating playlists was so powerful for me. I started listening to my favourite songs and even danced around the house when listening to them!

Rediscovering my love of reading has been a joy. I joined a book group of wonderful women who share a love of diverse books and come together every couple of months to chat about all things books. I have connected with new people online and face-to-face, and our shared love of books is the connection.

Getting Support for Doing This Work

To get a feeling of emotional safety around this self-discovery work, talk to some of "your people". These are the people who are happy for your development, celebrate your successes, want you to be well, and are there for you when you are not well. They can support you on this path and encourage you to keep going if you feel you are slipping into old habits.

If you are struggling to see your worth, ask your people. They will let you know why they love you and what they value about you.

I have a group of friends who nurture my self-discovery and who always encourage me to see my value. They love seeing me develop, change and evolve, and they embrace the new me that has emerged.

People Change and Evolve – It's Okay for You to Do This Too

It is important to be aware that people change throughout their lives. You may have come from a family where you weren't encouraged or allowed to change or develop. The version they knew of you, or the version they wanted you to be, was the version they always wanted you to remain.

"We are not obligated to stay the same. Our desires can change. Our identities can change. Our fields of interest can change. Our ideologies can change. Embracing our humanity means embracing the shifts that come with maturing. Change is not a fad. It's a normal part of life."

Minaa B, @minaa_b on Instagram

As you rediscover yourself and develop and change, it's about showing self-compassion to every facet of you. It's about gradually learning to accept and value yourself and opening your mind to new things. You will change further as you go through life, which is terrific.

I have changed so much in the years since my breakdown, and I am excited that I will continue to develop, change and evolve during the rest of my life.

I am now much stronger, I have boundaries, I value myself, I do things just for me, I put myself first, I don't try to fix things for others, and I don't spend my social time with people who aren't good for my mind, body and soul.

I do things that bring me joy. Practicing self-compassion is something I continue to do daily and I am much happier for it. I have rediscovered my sense of self – the naughty, funny, chatty, kind, loving soul that was always there but quashed. I embrace my sensitivity. I speak highly of myself without thinking it egotistical. I schedule in time just for me. I am so happy to be me now. It takes time and practice, but I do it because I know my worth.

These changes have had positive ripple effects on all who know me. They have encouraged me and my family to be much more open about our emotions and to communicate how we feel. Our communication has improved in every way.

Self-Discovery Led to My New Career

When I started to feel more confident, I took a course that allowed me to see what I wanted from life. I had been in a job that had brought me no joy for many years. I didn't know what to do next. I had lost my sense of self and self-worth and could not see what I would or could do other than the job I was familiar with.

Having experience of working in a variety of people-centred roles in the education field over twenty-five years, I knew my passion was to work with people who didn't value themselves and didn't feel like they belonged.

I trained as a coach with the Co-Active Training Institute. The training took longer than I anticipated due to ill health, but I completed it and am so glad I did. Coaching has given me purpose, motivation and drive again.

"A coach sees your potential and helps you become a better version of yourself."

Adam Grant

I believe wholeheartedly that you are the expert in your own life. Only you know your unique path through life. Only you know what you truly want. Only you know what works for you. I know that you are completely capable of finding the answers to whatever challenges you face. I know that you can treat yourself well.

It is hard to accept yourself when you haven't been allowed to be yourself, as life created you, but this is your time to start becoming the person you were always meant to be. Think about where you are in life today and where you want to be in the future. What is that thing you have always dreamed of?

Sometimes we need someone else to see the things we have forgotten in us, someone to guide us back to the things that used to bring us joy, to the ambitions we used to have. My coach did this for me. Because of my coach, I trained as a coach, I run my own business and am now writing this book.

Discovering yourself is worth it. It has many positive impacts on your life.

Once you really get to know yourself again, my hope is that you will value yourself so much that you won't change for anyone ever again and will live the rest of your life unapologetically you.

"May you never be subservient.

May you never prey to fitting in.

May you always swirl in all the directions the sacred winds want to take you.

May you never hush your laughter nor your tears.

May you breathe without restriction.

May you show up every single day to the calling that is you and may you always know the courage of your heart."

Fig Ally, *@figally on Instagram*

Ten Tips for Getting to Know Yourself

1. Start to become aware of how you currently see yourself and consider if/how you change yourself for others. Do this with kindness and compassion.
2. Reconnect with happy memories.
3. Think about people who you used to love spending time with.
4. Think about hobbies and activities that you used to love doing.
5. Reconnect with music and TV from happy times.
6. Make a scrapbook/journal of yourself. Get to know yourself and what you love.
7. Let "your people" know that you are doing this work.
8. Start to see that change is an essential part of life. All people change and grow. It is okay to change.
9. Get to know your wants and your dreams.
10. Live your life your way.

CHAPTER TWELVE
Healing Not Healed

"The best thing about rock bottom is the rock part. You discover the solid bit of you. The bit that can't be broken down further. The thing that you might sentimentally call a soul. At our lowest we find the solid ground of our foundation. And we can build ourselves anew."

Matt Haig,
The Comfort Book

Although I felt completely broken in August 2018, something inside me got me through. Something that helped me keep going to the next day and the next. Looking back, it was an inner strength. It must have been my foundation, as Matt Haig refers to it. Whatever "it" was, it drove me forward to get help, not to leave any stone unturned, to work hard on feeling better. There was so much about me that was wrong, that was struggling, that I was unhappy with, but I found an inner strength and determination to keep going.

Throughout this book, I have documented my healing path. You will find your path. Only you will know what is right for you, but I hope that some of my suggestions will give you a place to start. My wish is that sharing my experience in this book gives you hope.

At this moment, you may not feel strong, but you are. You are here, and you are reading this. You have something within you that will help you push forward. It may not feel like it now, but you have a foundation to build from. A motivation to start. A realisation that something needs to change.

Looking back, I realise that as I worked on my healing, there was a strong desire to be healed and fixed. This desire kept me going and made me very determined, but it was also detrimental to my health. Everything I did was with the goal of being fixed.

I signed up for many online courses, groups, and webinars. In my mind, each one was going to fix me. Each time I didn't feel fixed, my health was adversely affected. My mental health suffered. Things felt harder.

I was a perfectionist. I needed to get my healing right.

I came to realise that I thought in black and white. The only options I had at that point were to be ill or healed. There was no place in between. I put too much pressure on myself to be well (and not just well, but fixed).

What is Black and White Thinking?

Black and white thinking, or an all-or-nothing mindset, is a tendency to think in extremes, for example, seeing yourself as either a success or a failure with no middle ground.

Black and white thinking stops you from seeing the world as it is with a complete and vibrant range of colours. It prevents you from seeing that there is a middle ground. It evokes huge reactions which can affect you deeply. These reactions can affect your mental and physical well-being.

Many people think in black and white at some point, but for some it is the way they operate. They may know no other way. They may have been brought up by caregivers who viewed the world in black and white.

If you think in black and white, you are overly hard on yourself and are likely to be sensitive to criticism.

Words used in black and white thinking include should, always, never, and fail.

You may be a perfectionist – someone who strives for perfection and flawlessness, someone who is constantly putting pressure on themselves.

It is hard to forgive yourself or be self-compassionate if you think this way. Things are going well, or they aren't. There's no let-up in the way you push and criticise yourself.

If you realise this is how you think, try to be kind and gentle with yourself. You may have been hard on yourself for most of your life. You may have been pushing yourself to succeed and achieve all your life. This won't change overnight, but it can change.

You can learn to modify your way of thinking.

How to Move Away from Black and White Thinking

- Start to understand black and white thinking and become mindful of when you think this way.
- Become mindful of your language.
- Become aware of when you are hard on yourself when you are using these extremes and try to introduce

kinder and softer language Use words like "sometimes" or "yet" etc. For example, "I can't do it" becomes "I can't do it yet".

It's all about small and steady steps and softening the edges at first.

If you find yourself falling into black and white thinking in response to the actions of others, ask yourself these questions:

- Is what I am thinking true?
- Could there be another explanation? For example, when a friend tells you that they can't meet with you, rather than immediately think that the friend doesn't like you anymore, become curious as to whether there might be a valid reason why they can't see you.
- Reflect and ask yourself: "Has my brain taken me to the worst-case scenario?"

If it has, take some time out. Go for a walk or listen to some music.

Come back later and see if you view the situation slightly differently.

Try to create some distance between you and the emotion, e.g., rather than saying you are angry, say "I am feeling anger", and think about the cause. Are your emotions on high alert because you feel disappointed?

As you become more aware of your thinking patterns, you can reflect on whether you react or respond to things.

What is the Difference Between Reacting and Responding?

Reacting is quick, instant, emotional and without thought — often answering back.

Responding is when you hit the pause button, take your time, and consciously think about the next step before taking any action. Pausing allows you to see that there may be another side to the situation. It will enable you to step back and think about the emotions that are coming up for you.

It takes daily practice but now I can feel when I am reacting emotionally, and I press pause to allow myself time to calm down, breathe and think before I respond.

Healing is a Lifelong Journey

As I started to think from a more balanced perspective, I found my approach to my healing softened.

Moving away from wanting to be "fixed" or "healed" gave me a sense of relief and freedom. It took the pressure off and helped me be more compassionate.

I now see my healing as a lifelong journey of learning and growth. I am no longer looking to be healed. The hurting is less and less each day.

"…..healing is not like climbing a mountain, reaching the pinnacle, planting our flag, and resting on our achievement. It's more like following the spirals of a labyrinth toward the interior and back out again, over and over, until we have a deeper understanding of the same problems. We gain perspective and wisdom each time around."

Jen Miller, Quill of the Goddess
https://www.facebook.com/quillofthegoddess

Living Life in Colour

I now see life in a range of vibrant colours. Some days are colourful, some are dark, some are soothing, and some are vivid.

I know now that many colours are available to me, whatever my state of mind. I know that feelings are temporary and that things change. I know I can do this. I can get through the dark days. I have so much hope.

I no longer see myself within the limits of labels, for example, as a quiet person. I don't put limits on myself. I don't allow others to limit me by their limiting opinions. I know myself now. I am not just one thing or one trait. I am a whole range of vibrant colours.

The Me I Always Wanted to Be

The most wonderful part of my healing is that I have gotten to know myself more and more each day. After years of self-loathing, it has been quite the discovery to realise that I really like myself. I think I'm rather extraordinary actually!

My life has expanded in every way.

Pre-breakdown my life was small, narrow, closed, and limited. It lacked hope, and it certainly lacked fun and joy. Some of the people I spent most of my time and attention on were not good for my health. I allowed others' opinions of me to shape my life. I allowed others to make me feel small.

I now live life to the full. I have a completely different outlook on life. I feel a real sense of freedom. I smile more; I feel my feelings; I connect with the right people; I have boundaries that give me more time and space; I check in with my nervous system regularly; I know my values and needs; I put myself first. I trust myself. I make my own decisions without asking others for their approval or opinion. I no longer seek value from others. I know how to regulate my emotions and cut myself a lot of slack. Oh, and I swear more. You can't beat a bit of swear therapy!

It has taken a lot of hard work on my part to change the behaviours that I adopted during childhood.

I have had to learn:

- what a healthy relationship is
- how to feel my feelings

- how to set boundaries
- how to be my own cheerleader
- how to value and validate myself
- that not all people in my life were healthy for me
- how to treat me and all aspects of my life with self-compassion
- that I can speak up without feeling I am being rude.

I also wear dresses. I wear bright colours. I treat myself to colourful nails every fortnight. I dance around the kitchen.

These things may seem unusual or small to some, but to me, these are massive. I am not hiding anymore. I am happy to be seen. I am visible after years of being made to feel invisible and of also making myself invisible. I am proud of myself, and I proudly take up space now. I no longer shrink myself to fit places I've outgrown.

I have opened my mind to new things. I explore. I am adventurous. I connect with new people.

My health is so much better. I no longer have daily headaches, migraines, pelvic pain, and spinal, shoulder or neck pain.

My head is no longer crammed full of thoughts. I am, and always will be, an overthinker, but I recognise this now and am kinder to myself. I journal and have therapy to support me.

I appreciate my body and know how to listen to the messages my body is sending me.

I appreciate little Victoria in all her ages and stages and have a wonderful relationship with her.

I sleep better.

I am kinder to myself in every way.

It has taken a lot of hard work to get to the me of today. I have had to face my past and its effect on me. It has taken therapy, medication, homeopathy and other holistic treatments.

I have gone through many emotions about what happened and the significant people in my life. I have realised that my life is better and healthier without some people in it.

I now understand that I can't change people. However hard I try, some people will never see me, acknowledge me, like me or love me unconditionally. I choose not to give my energy to these people.

It has been a huge rollercoaster, but I have done, and am continuing to do, the hard work.

I am incredibly proud of myself.

"And once the storm is over, you won't remember how you made it through, how you managed to survive. You won't even be sure whether the storm is really over. But one thing is certain. When you come out of the storm, you won't be the same person who walked in. That's what this storm is all about."

Haruki Murakami

This quote resonates so much with me. I am very different to the me that was in my storm. I am still me, obviously, but I have changed immensely.

Sometimes I struggle to comprehend where I was in 2018 and how I got to today. Sometimes I don't know how I got through it all.

I was often hard on myself and didn't give myself the credit I deserved. I am learning that it's important to celebrate every win, however small. I am learning to celebrate my strength, my bravery and my perseverance.

I am generally really well now but I know that my healing is ongoing. I know that there will be triggers. But I also know how to look after myself during these times.

Triggers and Challenges

As you go through life, there will always be triggers and challenges. Triggers are the cues for danger – the things, people and situations that remind you of your past and what happened to you. Be kind to yourself when you experience these. Bring yourself back to the present moment and your breath.

The triggers that you encounter are your teachers. They show you what still needs to be healed.

You may have emotional scars, just like we have physical scars. You are human. What happened to you hurt you. It may have broken your heart. Be kind to yourself.

Activities that Support Healing

Here are some activities for you to try:

- Connect with people you love. People who make you feel good about yourself. People who are a joy to be around.
- When you are feeling unwell, write a gratitude journal. Appreciate the little things that are often taken for granted. This can feel hard when life is tough so don't put pressure on yourself.
- Journal your feelings.
- Meditate, do Yoga Nidra or Qigong.
- Shake and move those energies around your body.
- Stretch your body.
- Dance around the kitchen like no one's watching.
- Become aware of your nervous system and how you can regulate it.
- Check in with your body – do you have any aches and pains? Is your body sending you any messages? Listen to and honour those messages.
- Schedule some rest time – sit and just be (no phones!)
- Go for a walk.
- Focus on your needs.
- Have some time alone.
- Do creative activities.
- Do things that make you smile.
- Disconnect from the daily news if it distresses you.
- Unfollow accounts on social media that make you feel bad about yourself or trigger you.

Your Healing

The joy of healing is like an awakening in which you become mindful of how you treat yourself and want to be.

It is your chance to be the person you always wanted to be, to do what you have always wanted to do. To live. To be happy. To truly feel.

Let your healing become a daily practice.

Your healing is about honouring yourself and your needs, putting yourself first and treating yourself with kindness and compassion.

Here are some tips to help you implement healing in your daily life:

- Be intentional with your practice – make time for self-compassion every day.
- Create reminders – don't let this vital work slip. You deserve it.
- Become aware when you are slipping into your default behaviours. Don't beat yourself up. Self-compassion is key in developing your self-worth.
- Repeat daily affirmations that remind you of your value.

The goal in healing is to improve your relationship with yourself.

Your healing lies in you being in the driver's seat rather than your past and your trauma taking over.

Your healing lies in your realisation of how amazing you are, separate from those who made you feel otherwise.

It lies in offering yourself self-compassion.

It lies in you slowly and gently learning to accept yourself as you are.

It lies in you seeing your value.

All of this is possible for you.

You can do this.

You deserve to be happy.

You deserve to live life on your terms.

"Always remember you matter, you're important and you are loved, and you bring to this world things no one else can."

Charlie Mackesy,
The Boy, The Mole, The Fox and The Horse

Nine Tips for Supporting You on Your Life-long Healing Journey

1. Become mindful of your current ways of thinking. Do you think in extremes?
2. Learn about black and white thinking and how you can think in a more balanced way.
3. Try to take some pressure off yourself. Let yourself off the hook. Always treat yourself with compassion.
4. Find out more about reacting versus responding.
5. Practise taking a pause and responding rather than reacting.
6. Add healing practices into your daily life. Schedule them in, if this helps.
7. Always be compassionate if you feel your default behaviours/reactions returning.
8. Celebrate yourself and every step of your journey. You have got this.
9. As Melissa @mellowdoodles says on Instagram: **"Prioritise your peace. Every single time."**

Afterword

I hope this book has brought you a sense of peace and hope.

I hope it has helped you to see your absolute value.

I hope you feel like it is possible to make sense of your life and thrive.

———————

I run an online group programme alongside this book. It covers the content of the book in more depth with Zooms and peer support.

If you are not keen on group work, I am available for 1:1 coaching which will be tailored to you and your specific needs.

I also run peer support and private support groups to help people feel connected and less alone.

You can find out more about all my services via my website or my business pages on Facebook and Instagram:

https://www.withcompassion.co.uk/

Facebook – https://www.facebook.com/WithCompassionVictoria/

Instagram - https://www.instagram.com/withcompassion.coaching/

I am undertaking further research on emotional dysfunction within families, going no contact and estrangement for my second book.

I would like to connect with people who are thinking of going no contact with their birth family, or who are already estranged from their family, for research purposes.

If you would like to contact me, email me at:

victoria@withcompassion.co.uk

My aim is to make family estrangement less of a taboo subject and to garner more understanding and compassion for people who make this difficult decision.

With Compassion,

Victoria

References and Additional Resources

Introduction

Gruben, P (2016) *Umbilicus*, Paula Gruben

Postlethwait, N (2001) accessed 12 June 2022,
https://www.instagram.com/p/COEVs8ED7Fj/

Chapter 1 – Something's Not Right

Cantopher, Dr T (2012) *Depressive Illness, The Curse of the Strong*, 3rd edition 2012, Sheldon Press

Glouberman, Dr D (2002) *The Joy of Burnout - How the end of the world can be a new beginning,* Hodder and Stoughton

Northrup, C, MD, (2018) *Dodging Energy Vampires – an Empath's Guide to Evading Relationships that Drain You and Restoring your Health and Power,* Hay House Inc

Gibson, L C (2015) *Adult Children of Emotionally Immature Parents – How to Heal from Distant, Rejecting, or Self-Involved Parents,* New Harbinger

Lewis, C S (n.d.) accessed 25 Feb 2022,
https://www.goodreads.com/quotes/1034489-we-read-to-know-we-are-not-alone

Chapter 2 – The Power of Writing

Woolf, V (2020) *The Voyage Out, Dover Publications Ltd*

Codrington, K (2021) *Second Spring: The Self-Care Guide to the Menopause*, Harper Collins Publishers Ltd

Gibson, L C, PsyD (2021) *Self-Care for Adult Children of Emotionally Immature Parents,* New Harbinger

Harvard Health Publishing, Harvard Medical School (2011) *Writing about emotions may ease stress and trauma,* accessed 21 February 2022,
https://www.health.harvard.edu/healthbeat/writing-about-emotions-may-ease-stress-and-trauma

Angelou, M (2007) *I Know Why the Caged Bird Sings,* Virago Press

Please note - In my healing journey I sourced professional and medical help in the UK. In different countries around the world there will be different ways of sourcing help. Please follow the process appropriate for your country.

Chapter 3 – Reaching Out and Connecting on Social Media

Levine, P A (n.d.) *The Power of Connection to Heal Trauma*, accessed 10 March 2022,
https://kripalu.org/resources/power-connection-heal-trauma

Botwin, S (2019) *Thriving After Trauma, Stories of Living and Healing,* Rowman and Littlefield Publishers

Fitzgerald, L (2022), *Golden Questions*, accessed 12 March 2022,
https://www.facebook.com/therapydenonline/posts/pfbid0Hq

Y1xtjTdPDoqxhE44B5WUiMAfPcvKtEMDDsvXqsua7gptKF1ug1a
W4vUNLVsg8G

Hallowell, E.M. (1999) *Connect.* New York, NY: Pocket Books

Greenlee, G (2008) Postcards and Pearls: Life Lessons from Solo Moments on the Road, Aventine Press

Lou Lebentz and Trauma Thrivers - https://loulebentz.com/traumathrivers/ https://www.facebook.com/loulebentztraumathrivers/

Recommended Reading

Botwin, S (2019) *Thriving After Trauma: Stories of Living and Healing, Rowman & Littlefield Publishers*

Chapter 4 – Starting with a Whisper

Botwin, S (2019) *Thriving After Trauma: Stories of Living and Healing, Rowman & Littlefield Publishers*

Cantopher, Dr T (2012) *Depressive Illness, The Curse of the Strong*, 3rd edition, Sheldon Press

Mannix, K (2021) *Listen, How to Find the Words for Tender Conversations,* William Collins

Bernock, D (2014) Emerging With Wings: A True Story of Lies, Pain, And The LOVE that Heals, *2nd edition, 4F Medja*

Knost, L R (n.d.) shared by @Ravenous Butterflies on Facebook, accessed 21 March 2022, https://www.facebook.com/ravenous.butterflies

Recommended Reading

Mannix, K (2021) *Listen, How to Find the Words for Tender Conversations,* William Collins

Chapter 5 – Connecting with "Your" People

Dalai Lama, accessed 1 April 2022, https://www.goodreads.com/quotes/31335-we-human-beings-are-social-beings-we-come-into-thw

Rohn, J (n.d.) accessed 1 April 2022, https://www.goodreads.com/quotes/1798-you-are-the-average-of-the-five-people-you-spend

Angelou, M (n.d.) accessed 2 April 2022, https://www.goodreads.com/quotes/7532767-forgive-yourself-for-not-knowing-what-you-didn-t-know-before

Brown, B (2021) *Atlas of the Heart Mapping, Meaningful Connection and the Language of Human Experience,* Vermilion

Abdelnour, Z K (n.d.) accessed 2 April 2022, https://www.goodreads.com/quotes/971765-you-have-three-types-of-friends-in-life-friends-for

Gibson, L C, PsyD, (2021) *Self-Care for Adult Children of Emotionally Immature Parents,* New Harbinger

Margolyes, M (2021) *This Much is True,* John Murray

Chapter 6 – Seeking Professional Help

Diagram 1 – Gomez, Mily (2021) *How did the cup get full?* accessed 5 April 2022, https://www.instagram.com/p/CXeCR7cJln_/

Lebentz, L (2022) *The Phases of Trauma*, accessed 4 April 2022 https://www.instagram.com/p/CaT09qaMRLf

Diagram 2 - Lebentz, L (2022) *The Phases of Trauma*, accessed 4 April 2022 https://www.instagram.com/p/CaT09qaMRLf

UK Council for Psychotherapy (n.d.) accessed 5 April 2022, https://www.psychotherapy.org.uk/seeking-therapy/what-is-psychotherapy

Briant-Smith, A (2022) *What is Homeopathy?* posted 16 February 2022, accessed 5 April 2022, https://www.facebook.com/HomeopathAbi

The Reiki Council (2015) accessed 5 April 2022, https://www.reikicouncil.org.uk/What-is-Reiki.php

Shaman Durek, accessed 5 April 2022, https://shamandurek.com/shamanic/shamanic-healing/

EFT International, accessed 6 April 2022, https://eftinternational.org/discover-eft-tapping/what-is-eft-tapping/

Trauma Thrivers Private Group on Facebook - https://www.facebook.com/groups/traumathrivers

Asta, C (2021) *To all the people who are working on their healing*, accessed 4 April 2022, https://www.instagram.com/p/CW_Zuccsxkd

Additional Resources

You can find out about other trauma therapies and treatments on Lou Lebentz's Instagram page –
https://www.instagram.com/traumathrivers_loulebentz/

Lou is also on Facebook –
https://www.facebook.com/loulebentztraumathrivers/

You can try EFT on the following YouTube channels:

https://www.youtube.com/c/tapwithbrad

https://www.youtube.com/c/JulieSchiffman1

https://www.findahomeopath.org/what-is-homeopathy

Please note - In my healing journey I sourced professional and medical help in the UK. In different countries there will be different ways of sourcing professional and medical help. Please follow the process appropriate for your country.

Chapter 7 – An Introduction to the Mind-Body Connection and the Nervous System

Bessel A. van der Kolk (2015) The Body Keeps the Score: Brain, Mind, and Body in the Healing of Trauma, 1st Edition, Penguin

Unknown, accessed 14 April 2022,
https://www.pinterest.co.uk/pin/if-you-listen-to-your-body-when-it-whispers-you-wont-have-to-hear-it-scream--381539399684656164

Rawlinson, A (2020) Listen to Your Body, accessed 14 April 2022 @therapywithabby,
https://www.instagram.com/p/CGzifooDLvN

Friedman-Gell,L, PHD and Barron J PSYD (2020) *Intergenerational Trauma Workbook; Strategies to Support Your Journey of Discovery, Growth and Healing*, Rockridge Press

Porges, Dr S, https://www.stephenporges.com

Diagram 1 – Rawlinson, A (2021) *The Autonomic Ladder*, accessed 14 April 2022 @therapywithabby, https://www.instagram.com/p/CO0UQgRjjJ9

Dennis R (2021) *Let It Go, Breathe Yourself Calm,* Happy Place Books

Maguire, J, accessed 15 April 2022, https://www.instagram.com/repairing_the_nervous_system/

Additional Resources

Dana, D (2020) *Polyvagal Exercises for Safety and Connection*, Norton

Mate, Dr G (2019) *When the Body Says No, The Cost of Hidden Stress*, Penguin Random House

Rothschild, B (2010) *8 Keys to Safe Trauma Recovery, Take-Charge Strategies to Empower Your Healing*, Norton

Jessica Maguire, Repairing the Nervous System - https://www.instagram.com/repairing_the_nervous_system/

Marina YT, Compassionate Somatic Coach - https://www.instagram.com/marina.y.t/

Anna the Anxiety Coach - https://www.instagram.com/annatheanxietycoach/

Rebecca Dennis, Breathing Tree – https://www.instagram.com/breathing.tree/

You can find Rebecca's breathwork exercises on YouTube. This is one example -
https://www.youtube.com/watch?v=Ga3WY8djVvl

Therapy with Abby -
https://www.instagram.com/therapywithabby/

Chapter 8 – Learning How to Feel

Friedman-Gell,L, PHD and Barron J PSYD (2020) *Intergenerational Trauma Workbook; Strategies to Support Your Journey of Discovery, Growth and Healing, Rockridge Press*

David, S (2017) *Emotional Agility, Get Unstuck, Embrace Change and Thrive in Work and Life,* Penguin

Brown, B (2021), List of Emotions, accessed 21 April 2022, https://brenebrown.com/resources/atlas-of-the-heart-list-of-emotions

Brown, B (2021) *Atlas of the Heart Mapping, Meaningful Connection and the Language of Human Experience,* Vermilion

Doyle Dr G, (2021) Naming an Emotion, accessed 24 April 2022, https://www.instagram.com/p/CT_S7pgM5zy/

Sark (2022), *If she got really quiet and listened*, accessed 20 May 2022, https://www.facebook.com/PlanetSARK/posts/pfbid034aNDw4LSFyjgVuumRdzmqNhPWAEdRRyADG1t2FT1Zr87gv1mSscDHdheo9pXAoGKl

Additional Resources

Susan David - https://www.instagram.com/susandavid_phd/

Brene Brown - https://www.instagram.com/brenebrown/

Dr Glenn Doyle - https://www.instagram.com/drdoylesays/

Brackett, M, PhD. (2019) *Permission to Feel: Unlocking the Power of Emotions to Help Our Kids, Ourselves, and Our Society Thrive*, Celadon Books

Chapter 9 – Moving from People-Pleasing to Setting Boundaries

@junocounselling, post accessed 2 May 2002, https://www.instagram.com/junocounselling

You can see more work from Dr Emma Hepburn @ThePsychologyMum on Instagram – https://www.instagram.com/thepsychologymum

Quote from Brittin Oakman, seen on *The Artidote* Facebook page, accessed 4 May 2022, https://www.facebook.com/theartidote

Read more about the seven different types of rest on:

https://blog.ed.ted.com/2021/02/08/the-7-types-of-rest-that-every-person-needs/?msclkid=4740b4f6cfa811ec9e79aa3f7592b3f6

Scher, A B (2021) *How to Heal Yourself From Depression When No One Else Can,* Sounds True

Ernst, J (2002) *The Five Types of Boundaries*, accessed 4 May 2022, https://www.instagram.com/p/CaqlMiaOtsw/

Rawlinson, A (2002) *Signs You Might Need to Tighten Your Boundaries*, accessed 4 May 2022 @therapywithabby, https://www.instagram.com/p/CZMnyemM0iT/

Kerry Dunn @people.pleasers.rehab Instagram Story, accessed 6 May 2022,
https://www.instagram.com/people.pleasers.rehab/

Davis, M (posted 14 March 2022) *I am Safe Inside Myself*, Accessed 6 May 2022,
https://www.facebook.com/WildGooseCounseling

Tawwab, N G (2021) *Set Boundaries, Find Peace, A Guide to Reclaiming Yourself*, Piatkus

Additional Resources

Tawwab, N G (2021) *The Set Boundaries Workbook, Practical Exercises for Understanding Your Needs and Setting Healthy Limits*, Piatkus

Nedra Glover Tawwab -
https://www.instagram.com/nedratawwab/

People Pleasers Rehab –
https://www.instagram.com/people.pleasers.rehab/

Wild Goose Counseling –
https://www.facebook.com/WildGooseCounseling

Sana Powell - https://www.instagram.com/curly_therapist/

Chapter 10 – Opening your Heart to Self-Compassion

Neff, K, PhD and Germer,C, PhD (2018) *The Mindful Self-Compassion Workbook, A Proven Way to Accept Yourself, Build Inner Strength, and Thrive, 1st Edition*, Guilford Press

Kimsey-House, H, Kimsey-House, Sandahl, K, Whitworth L (2018) *Co-Active Coaching, The Proven Framework for*

Transformative Conversations at Work and in Life, 4th Edition, Nicholas Brealey Publishing

Friedman-Gell,L, PHD and Barron J PSYD (2020) *Intergenerational Trauma Workbook; Strategies to Support Your Journey of Discovery, Growth and Healing, Rockridge Press*

Neff, K (2021) *Fierce Self-Compassion, How Women Can Harness Kindness to Speak Up, Claim Their Power and Thrive,* Penguin Life

Fitzgerald, L, Values Exercise adapted from a course undertaken by the author in 2021 You can find out more about Lori at - https://www.facebook.com/therapydenonline

Neff, K (n.d.) Take the Self-Compassion Test: https://self-compassion.org/self-compassion-test/

Angelou, M, Accessed 14 May 2022, Available at https://www.relicsworld.com/maya-angelou/i-learned-a-long-time-ago-the-wisest-thing-i-can-do-author-maya-angelou

Additional Resources

Resources on Kristin Neffs's website:

- https://self-compassion.org/category/exercises/#exercises
- https://self-compassion.org/category/exercises/#guided-meditations
- https://self-compassion.org/videos/

Kristin Neff - https://www.instagram.com/neffselfcompassion/

Hayley Kaye - https://www.instagram.com/iamhayleykaye/

My website – https://www.withcompassion.co.uk/

Chapter 11 – Getting to Know Yourself

Gibson, L C, PsyD (2019) *Recovering from Emotionally Immature Parents, Practical Tools to Establish Boundaries and Reclaim Your Emotional Autonomy,* New Harbinger

McDowell, E, accessed 15th May 2022, https://www.goodreads.com/quotes/9586181-finding-yourself-is-not-really-how-it-works-you-aren-t

Minaa B (2022) *We Are Not Obligated to Stay the Same*, accessed 28th May 2022, https://www.instagram.com/p/CcX66jDOfFB/

Grant, A (2021) *It's easy to be a critic or a cheerleader. It's harder to be a coach*, accessed 28th May 2022, https://twitter.com/adammgrant/status/14602599748237475 89?lang=en-G

Fig Ally (n.d.) Accessed 29th May 2022, https://m.facebook.com/Kaaiomeditation/photos/may-you-never-be-subservient-may-you-never-fall-prey-to-fitting-in-may-you-alway/199449715298683

Fig Ally can also be found on Instagram - https://www.instagram.com/figally

Chapter 12 – Healing Not Healed

Haig, M (2021) *The Comfort Book, Canongate Books*

Miller, J (2022) accessed 4 June 2002,

https://www.facebook.com/quillofthegoddess/posts/pfbid06 WXZ1eFJZ HgXtQRyEv1ycFm6YKhf8io99Yqpjsq4EaVvAMn2MK258jtf9nhR Yut2

Murakami, H (n.d.) accessed 5 June 2022, https://www.goodreads.com/quotes/315361-and-once-the-storm-is-over-you-won-t-remember-how

Melissa (2021) accessed 5 June 2022, https://www.instagram.com/p/CWymkDUo1Me/

Mackesy, C (2019) *The Boy, The Mole, The Fox and The Horse*, Ebury Press

Additional Resources

LePera N Dr (2021) *How To Do The Work, Recognise Your Patterns, Heal From Your Past + Create Your Self*, Dr Nicole LePera, 1st Edition, Orion Spring

The Holistic Psychologist - https://www.instagram.com/the.holistic.psychologist/

Rebekah Ballagh - https://www.instagram.com/journey_to_wellness_/

Sana Powell - https://www.instagram.com/curly_therapist/

Books that I Found Useful in My Healing

Botwin, S (2019) Thriving After Trauma, Stories of Living and Healing, Rowman and Littlefield Publishers

Brach, T (2003) Radical Acceptance, Awakening the Love that Heals Fear and Shame, Rider Books

Brackett, M, PhD. (2019) Permission to Feel: Unlocking the Power of Emotions to Help Our Kids, Ourselves, and Our Society Thrive, Celadon Books

Brown, B (2021) Atlas of the Heart Mapping, Meaningful Connection and the Language of Human Experience, Vermilion

Cantopher, Dr T (2012) Depressive Illness, The Curse of the Strong, 3ʳᵈ edition 2012, Sheldon Press

Codrington, K (2021) Second Spring: The Self-Care Guide to the Menopause, Harper Collins Publishers Ltd

Dana, D (2020) Polyvagal Exercises for Safety and Connection, Norton

David, S (2017) Emotional Agility, Get Unstuck, Embrace Change and Thrive in Work and Life, Penguin

Friedman-Gell,L, PHD and Barron J PSYD (2020) Intergenerational Trauma Workbook; Strategies to Support Your Journey of Discovery, Growth and Healing, Rockridge Press

Gibson, L C (2015) Adult Children of Emotionally Immature Parents – How to Heal from Distant, Rejecting, or Self-Involved Parents, New Harbinger

Gibson, L C, PsyD (2019) Recovering from Emotionally Immature Parents, Practical Tools to Establish Boundaries and Reclaim Your Emotional Autonomy, New Harbinger

Gibson, L C, PsyD (2021) Self-Care for Adult Children of Emotionally Immature Parents, New Harbinger

Glouberman, Dr D (2002) The Joy of Burnout - How the end of the world can be a new beginning, Hodder and Stoughton

Guzman, L, ATR-BC (2020) Essential Art Therapy Exercises, Effective Techniques to Manage Anxiety, Depression, and PTSD, Rockridge Press

LePera N Dr (2021) How To Do The Work, Recognise Your Patterns, Heal From Your Past + Create Your Self, Dr Nicole LePera, 1 Edition, Orion Spring

Mate, Dr G (2019) When the Body Says No, The Cost of Hidden Stress, Penguin Random House

Mellody, P with Wells Miller, A and Miller, JK (2003) Facing Codependence, What It Is, Where It Comes From, How It Sabotages Our Lives, Harper One

Neff, K (2021) Fierce Self-Compassion, How Women Can Harness Kindness to Speak Up, Claim Their Power and Thrive, Penguin Life

Neff, K (2011) Self-Compassion, the Proven Power of Being Kind to Yourself, Yellow Kite

Neff, K, PhD and Germer,C, PhD (2018) The Mindful Self-Compassion Workbook, A Proven Way to Accept Yourself, Build Inner Strength, and Thrive, 1 Edition, Guilford Press

Northrup, C, MD, (2018) Dodging Energy Vampires – an Empath's Guide to Evading Relationships that Drain You and Restoring your Health and Power, Hay House Inc

Rothschild, B (2010) 8 Keys to Safe Trauma Recovery, Take-Charge Strategies to Empower Your Healing, Norton

Tawwab, N G (2021) Set Boundaries, Find Peace, A Guide to Reclaiming Yourself, Piatkus

Bessel A. van der Kolk (2015) The Body Keeps the Score: Brain, Mind, and Body in the Healing of Trauma, 1st Edition, Penguin

Wolynn, M (2016) It Didn't Start With You, How Inherited Family Trauma Shapes Who We Are And How To End The Cycle, Penguin

Social media accounts I found useful:

Mental and Emotional Health

Catherine Asta –
https://www.instagram.com/catherine.asta/

Minaa B - https://www.instagram.com/minaa_b/

Jake Ernst - https://www.instagram.com/mswjake/

Lori Fitzgerald, The Therapy Den –
https://www.facebook.com/therapydenonline

Whitney Goodman - https://www.instagram.com/sitwithwhit/

Hearts of Growth –
https://www.instagram.com/heartsofgrowth/

New Happy Co - https://www.instagram.com/newhappyco/

The Psychology Mum –
https://www.instagram.com/thepsychologymum/

Real Depression Project -
https://www.instagram.com/realdepressionproject/

Trauma

Dr Glenn Doyle – https://www.instagram.com/drdoylesays/

Emmy Marie –
https://www.instagram.com/bloomingwithemmy/

Lou Lebentz Trauma Thrivers –
https://www.facebook.com/loulebentztraumathrivers/

Lou Lebentz – https://loulebentz.com
https://www.instagram.com/traumathrivers_loulebentz

Mel Curtis - https://www.instagram.com/meltalkstrauma/

Shari Botwin - https://www.facebook.com/shari.botwin

Family dysfunction and trauma

Family Support Resources -
https://www.instagram.com/familysupportresources/

Laura K Connell - https://www.instagram.com/laurakconnell/

Dr Nicole LePera -
https://www.instagram.com/the.holistic.psychologist/

Sleep

Stephanie Sleep Expert –
https://www.instagram.com/stephsleepyhead/

About the Author

Victoria Matthews-Patel is a Compassionate Coach, Mentor, and Mental Health First Aider. She is Co-Author of My Voice, Journeys of Survival, Empowerment and Self-Compassion.

Victoria's 25 years of work in the education and charity sectors involved supporting, mentoring, teaching, training, managing and coaching people of all ages, especially those who felt they were struggling or who had low self-worth.

Victoria is also a trauma survivor and thriver. After years of ill mental and physical health, she had a breakdown in 2018. With professional help, she uncovered layers of hidden trauma.

She trained as a coach in 2020-2021 and now runs a coaching and mentoring business, With Compassion, championing people who grew up in emotionally dysfunctional families.

Compassion is at the heart of all her work.

Victoria is a wife and a Mum to a wonderful daughter. She loves nothing more than going for a walk in nature with her gorgeous dog, curling up with a good book, singing with Rock Choir, writing and journalling. Going to concerts and the theatre, eating out, travel and connecting with "her" people bring her so much joy.

She fully embraces life now and continues to work on her healing every day.

You can connect with Victoria at:

Website
https://www.withcompassion.co.uk/contact-victoria/

Facebook
https://www.facebook.com/WithCompassionVictoria/

Instagram
https://www.instagram.com/withcompassion.coaching/

LinkedIn
https://www.linkedin.com/in/victoria-matthews-patel-a43568104/

YouTube
https://www.youtube.com/@victoriamatthews-patel

Lightning Source UK Ltd.
Milton Keynes UK
UKHW010707300123
416172UK00001B/94